AF480002

Thank you to Mark Warner and the team at Martial Journal for partnering with us for the Modern Moms of Martial Arts project.

Scan the QR code below to check out this free online martial arts magazine.

If you would like to write for Martial Journal, use the contact form on the website.

AVAILABLE FROM WHISTLEKICK BOOKS PUBLISHING

BY JEREMY LESNIAK

Non-Fiction

The Martial Artist's Handbook

12 Months to Health

How Not to Hold a Tournament

Stronger people Are Harder to Kill

Press Release Mastery

Simpler Social Media

Starting to Sell on Amazon

Fiction

Faith: The Katana Chronicles - Book One

The Katana Chronicles - Book Two **COMING SOON!**

BY JENNI SIU

The Origin of Master Hopkick: Beginnings

The Origin of Master Hopkick: Beginnings - Special Edition

The Origin of Master Hopkick: Beginnings - Instructor's Edition (w/ Chris Rickard)

The Origin of Master Hopkick: Lessons

The Origin of Master Hopkick Book Three **COMING SOON!**

BY CHRIS RICKARD

The Instructor's Guide to Jenni Siu's The Origin of Master Hopkick: Beginnings - Mat Chat and Classroom Discussion Guide

BY JENNI NATHER

Modern Moms of Martial Arts: Volume One

INSPIRED BY WHISTLEKICK MARTIAL ARTS RADIO

Collections

Celebrating Women in the Martial Arts
Legends of the Martial Arts
What Advice Would You Give Martial Artists 100 Years From Now?
A Journey Into the Badlands w/ Daniel Wu, Emily Beecham, and Sherman Augustus
The Karate Kid & Cobra Kai Collection
Restomp The Interviews w/ Master ken, Matt page, and Joseph Conway

One-on-One Interviews

Tony Blauer
Mr. Don "The Dragon" Wilson
Shihan Bas Rutten
Bill "superfoot" Wallace
Adrian Paul
Sensei Fumio Demura
Iain Abernethy
Five Faces of Kempo
Jhoon Rhee
Stephen Hayes
Nathan Porter

SEARCH US ON AMAZON FOR MORE TITLES!

wK Books

Modern Moms of Martial Arts

Volume One

WRITTEN BY JENNI NATHER AND FRIENDS
COVER ART BY ZEE SOFFRON

wK Books

Original Cover Art by Zee Soffron ©2024

Dedication

This book is dedicated to my greatest accomplishments and the reasons why I am a mom: Cade, Mason, Tannim, and Lilith.

Mama is proud of you all. You are amazing, loving, strong human beings. Keep reaching for your dreams.

I'll always have your back.

Contents

Introduction

I was hurting. I even felt like a failure. I had to work full-time, so I didn't have the time to be the perfect mom, but I sacrificed my own needs to try anyway.

I often felt that it was so easy for other moms, so something must be wrong with me. Maybe I wasn't cut out for motherhood because I "should" have been able to do all the amazing things I saw other moms doing. Why did they all seem so good at this?

I suffered in silence as I tried to put on a show to fit in with the moms who seemed to always have time to cook from scratch every day, attend every school event for each of their kids, complete DIY projects, and volunteer at the school and sporting events, all while keeping their homes clean and organized, making sure everyone made it to all doctors' appointments and activities, and still having enough time for Family Game Night.

Slowly, I bravely opened up to other moms about the struggles I faced, and thank goodness I did. I learned that I was not only doing better than I thought, but I also now knew I was not alone. Like me, other moms felt like they couldn't talk about their struggles and failures for fear of judgment.

Some of my great co-workers at whistlekick suggested that the topic of moms who train in martial arts would make a great book, and I knew instantly that they were right.

This project would help all moms, not just the martial moms. (Although, I'd be lying if I said I didn't secretly hope that all moms would be encouraged to train.)

This project would make other moms aware that they have a community to support them and cheer them on. We could stop "shoulding" ourselves and be confident that we were doing great.

I put out the call for other moms like me who wanted to help remove the stigma of what society leads us to believe a mom "should" be.

The responses I received tell me that we all agree – moms need this love and support, and we are ready to lift each other up. We are finished with trying to live up to some ideal that requires us to sacrifice too much of ourselves.

I cried seeing the responses to the call, and I cried again seeing what we created together. I am deeply moved, and I feel so connected to you all.

I couldn't help but notice through our stories that each of us demonstrated in our own ways that we wanted to do the best we could for our families and that we all needed help to do that. I feel stronger and more confident after reading these stories, so I can't wait to help other moms out there feel the same way.

Moms helping other moms is so important and so necessary that I plan to continue to put out additional volumes of *Modern Moms of Martial Arts*. If you would like to submit your story for the next volume of *Modern Moms of Martial Arts*, email me at books@whistlekick.com.

Thank you to my fellow martial arts moms who shared their stories. I know we are making a difference for other moms out there.

To all moms, you are awesome. You are doing great. You are not alone.

I am so proud of you.

~Jenni Nather

Modern Moms of Martial Arts

"This is motherhood for you," said my own mother. "Going through life with your heart outside your body."

Jennifer Weiner

The Martial Art of Motherhood: A Kung Fu

Run any two projects side-by-each. See what they share? A practice, an approach, or an opportunity to excel slips over the boundary between them.

My daughter began her martial arts practice at my insistence. Just beginning middle school, she was smart, nerdy even, and a bit emo. She was also bullied. One morning as she stepped toward the school bus, shoulders up and eyes dropped to the pavement, a small gold car swerved around the bus. It missed her by three feet. I suddenly saw her as she was: too alone, too unprotected. Even though she started training reluctantly, she was strong and well-coordinated.

I would watch. Or I would grocery shop and return to pick her up. Or I would sit out front of the dojo reading. One afternoon, deep into a book, I glanced up to see an eight-year-old sitting beside me flipping through a picture book. Our children look to us for how to live their lives. I needed to model dedication or even just how to have fun for my daughter. Although I was not strong or coordinated, I started training shortly after. I chose classes close to her schedule so we could spend the few minutes between watching each other.

> Suggestion 1: Adjust your schedule AND your
> thinking. What if your child is better at certain skills
> than you? This is a wonderful opportunity for your
> child to gain confidence and for you to step back.
> There will be a day when your child can outperform
> you, even simply based on age. Take some time to see
> how this feels.

Then we began training on Friday nights. Friday night is a
lonely night for a young teenager. Neither they nor their
friends can drive. When I was a girl, my father took me and
my siblings to the YMCA every Friday night for the open
swim. Back then, we spent the entire two hours diving,
racing, and holding our breath as long as possible as we swam
underwater. With my daughter, even in different classes, we
took the time away from school and work pressures to play
and laugh and end the work week out of the house.

> Suggestion 2: Make training time a time away from
> daily pressures. Even if you get to coordinate with
> only one class each week, make that one special by
> finding a way to share the experience.

The year my daughter graduated from high school was the
year we earned black belts together. No longer just there for
the workout, both of us had to focus on the art we were
practicing; she, Kempo, and me, Muay Thai. The older she
got, the more options she had for social activities, but still she
kept coming, as I kept coming. For her, that goal would be
met just before she went off to college; for me, that goal
would be met just before she left home. We celebrated
together.

> Suggestion 3: A shared accomplishment is so sweet.
> Recognize how both of you grew during your time
> training together.

While she was away, believing more in my abilities, I took on harder jobs at work. I added other styles to my practice and eventually focused on Shaolin and Northern Mantis. In college, my daughter switched to fencing to keep up her sword skills and expand her range. Once, in the middle of her sophomore year, a friend of hers in the midst of a breakdown swung at her. She didn't flinch.

> Suggestion 4: Even if one or both of you move on to
> other arts or life experiences, participate in seminars
> or special classes to expand your skills and knowledge
> of the arts. These are days you will continue to
> treasure.

Place any mother and child side-by-each. Watch how they move. Check when they smile. See what they share?

Donna French McArdle

A warrior believes in an end she can't see and fights for it. A warrior never gives up. A warrior fights for those weaker than herself. It sounds like motherhood to me.

Kristin Hannah, "The Four Winds"

Karate Journey

Growing up, I was an athlete year-round – soccer or
volleyball in the fall, basketball in the winter, and softball in
the spring and into the summer with my town league. I was
always active, riding my bike everywhere, running around
with friends, your "typical" Gen X kid. I was competitive, I
wanted to win and beat myself up when we lost. I wanted to
be the best.

Off to college in 1995, I discovered rowing and fell in love
with the sport, the water, the rush, everything. I worked out
two, sometimes three times a day. I traveled to warmer
climates in the winter just to get my fix of the water. I helped
coach novice teams, competed in international events, and
even attempted to try out for the national rowing team (I was
too short at 5'8"). I continued for 10 years until I didn't. One
day I woke up and I was done. No more sports, no more
games, meets, regattas, nothing. I was tired, my body ached,
and my shoulder was plagued with the beginning of
osteoarthritis. I was burnt out. I switched my focus to my
career as a pastry chef and just looked ahead.

Fast forward a decade or so. I was married, had two boys,
and a great career as a pastry chef. Unfortunately, my

happiness came with a crazy shift in my weight and physical fitness. It was getting harder and harder to keep up with two boys and work without collapsing on the couch at night. I craved that feeling you get after a good workout but was so scared to start again. I found some videos, bought a knockoff Peloton bike, and started working out again. With my husband's help, we started eating better as well, and slowly, I began to feel better.

Then came 2020 …

My family, like most, tried to stay as active as possible but the stress of an unknown disease, homeschooling, and still working out of the home definitely took its toll, and this is how my martial arts journey really began.

My boys started karate as the world learned to "live with" COVID back in February of 2021. In Boston, we were masking, social distancing, and hand sanitizing, but my God, the boys needed to get out of the house! A local dojo that has been around for 40 years seemed like a great option since flag football, soccer, and baseball were not something either boy was into! So, at 5 and 9 we joined the "One Step Beyond" family. They LOVED it, begged to go more, and quickly advanced in belts.

Next came the weapons. Henry (5) started bo and Alex (9) took up kamas. I was at the dojo 3-4 times a week. I brought work, knitting, and books and sat through class after class for nearly two years. Occasionally Sensei Marie McKenna would chat with me before or after class. We had some things in common – both athletes during our teen and young adult years, her sport being soccer, and she turned her passion for fitness into a full-time job, and later took up karate in her 40s with her boys in tow. Later, she took over the dojo with a fellow black belt student after the owner moved. She would encourage me to participate but I always had an excuse. I was still working out at home, slowly shedding COVID pounds, but horribly intimidated to work out in front of anyone. It wasn't until my husband started helping my son with sparring that I even considered coming to class.

In September of 2022, I caved and took my first class. Having recently switched jobs, I was in a better spot mentally and wanted to "move" again as my knockoff Peloton bike just wasn't cutting it. I loved it, the kicks, strikes, movement, everything. I religiously attended class with my husband. The kids would hang with the Sensei's kids and we all eventually became very close.

As my oldest trained with a Kama coach in Texas via Zoom with me recording and watching every move, I realized my youngest was feeling a little "left out". In January 2023, I asked Sensei Erin Smith if she would train me on bo so I could help Henry. One class in and I was hooked. We worked a simple form and in March 2023 I competed in my first tournament, kids cheering me on.

At my second tournament, as I was getting scored, I looked over to the ring to my right and there was Alex, who received 9.99s across the board – his first, first place – and between my ring and his was my husband and son Henry, cheering us both on! The look on Alex's face was priceless, he worked so hard for that moment.

By the summertime, the whole family was traveling and competing in local tournaments. Granted I never had anyone to compete against (not many 40-plus underbelts) but due to my advancing skill and determination, Sensei Erin "surprised" me at Amerikick in NJ by entering me in the 40-plus black belt division! I dropped due to nerves, placed 1st against one other competitor, and even got to grands – overall a great experience!

Fast forward to 2024, we still all train together, compete together, and support our amazing dojo family. My husband and I help out when the Senseis compete in larger tournaments and WKC, and our boys are close with Sensei Marie's boys still. Each tournament we get better, sometimes place a little higher, but most importantly learn a little something new about ourselves.

As I write this, recovering from a cold, sore from practice last night (oh, I needed to get out of the house!), I realize it might be the oldest cliché to say that "age is just a number" or "you're never too old to learn something new," but it's 100% true. Karate brought me back to those feelings I had in my 20s, the rush of competing, being on a team, striving to be a better version of oneself, but now being older and a little wiser and with my family, it's fulfilling and brings a sense of peace and balance to my life. Karate is my family, both blood and dojo born.

Jennifer Luna

*Sometimes the strength of
motherhood is greater than natural
laws.*

Barbara Kingsolver, "Homeland and Other Stories"

Never Give Up on Your Journey

When I first entered the karate dojo I thought of all the possible new things I could learn. My first introduction to karate was taking a kickboxing class for exercise. I loved punching and kicking the bags and that every class had similar routines, but was also different depending on what instructor was teaching the class. At first, I was just going to the dojo not even considering myself as a martial artist, instead just to meet new people and exercise. When I became pregnant with my first child, I continued class until I could no longer attend and became a full-time mother. I wanted to go back to kickboxing, but would have to wait a couple of years until I found the time and energy to push myself to start again. Kickboxing was always my outlet, which helped me stay in shape and deal with stress at the same time.

After my first child was born, it took a while to get adjusted to being a mother and caring for this new person. Going back to work part-time, I wanted to return to kickboxing for my exercise routine. Starting my classes again was just what I needed. I soon learned that a coworker of mine was taking karate classes at the school where I was taking my kickboxing class. I was interested in going with him to check out the class and see if karate was something I would enjoy. I felt very insecure in this new class, something I had never thought of trying out before, but I felt it was an art that I would enjoy learning and I felt comfortable with the group of people at the dojo. Everyone was there to make themselves better, but also willing to help others learn and grow together. For myself, karate would have to wait a few years in order to start my martial arts journey.

As the years went by, my oldest son was growing fast and had some behavioral issues beginning at school, mainly focusing and acting out when frustrated. One day as my kickboxing class was ending, I noticed the kids lining up on the mats to begin their karate class. I thought to myself that karate may be good for my son. I went home to talk about it with my husband. Our son was never into team sports even though we tried soccer at a young age. I felt karate would expose him to a group of people who all had different reasons for taking classes and making themselves better. I thought it would teach him discipline and set goals for his future life, to always try and learn new things and become better every day. Within a few weeks, we had him signed up to begin karate class.

At the beginning, it was a struggle to get him to class as I was rushing to leave work, get him ready, and get to the 4:30 class. Every class he would learn new techniques and lessons. I would enjoy watching him on the mats and talking with the other parents. Every couple of months belt testing would take place on Saturday mornings. This was an exciting time and the instructors would test the kids on what curriculum was needed for each belt rank. After the one-hour testing session, the parents were invited back into the dojo and they would have graduation and announce the kids that had passed their test and earned a new belt. As the years went by, my son was enjoying karate and became a brown belt. Now the real learning began, as my son would now relearn the curriculum from each belt and perfect his skills to test for his black belt. My son truly grew through this time and has fond memories of people he has met during his classes.

In between the years, while my oldest was learning karate, my husband also began karate classes. He was having back issues and thought karate would help with flexibility and strengthening his back. Through many years and many classes, his back had less pain and he is now training to test for his third-degree Sensei rank in July of this year. My husband and oldest son received their first-degree black belts together about seven years ago. As I was spending more time at the dojo watching them training and participating in tournaments and seminars, I began to think our younger son would also benefit from karate. We signed him up at age 4 to the Rangers program, the beginner class, before being a white belt. It was so great seeing him in his small gi uniform following what his instructors were teaching him. My younger son too grew fast and enjoyed going to class and meeting new friends. Now looking back at all the years that have passed it is amazing to see how the two boys have grown up so much and the different personalities they both have.

Many days were spent at the dojo watching the boys learn new drills, new takedowns, and sparring on Friday nights. As time went by I too developed back pain spasms that would limit me from doing exercise. My husband thought that if I tried karate maybe I too could benefit from the flexibility and help relieve the pain I was having in my back. The moment I started class I was hooked and wanted to keep going to class while learning new techniques. I had met a group of adults and we all would enjoy class and make each other better. My whole family was taking karate together and at times we would all be in the same class as a family. Sometimes even my husband was teaching a class and I would have to say "Yes Sir" to him. That only happened on the mats in the dojo! It was a great feeling to be all together and we formed a nice relationship with our karate dojo.

A few struggles happened on the way. Beginning my training as a white belt, my back would have spasms. Sometimes in the middle of class, I would have muscle spasms and I would just push myself through the class. The more I pushed through and got more flexible the spasms would be less frequent. I believe the spasms were due to stiffness and weakness in my back muscles. Karate, kickboxing and just getting up and moving really helped strengthen my core. Sometimes we believe that when we injure ourselves we should rest. However, if you keep stretching and pushing through the pain the body will eventually heal itself. A positive attitude also always helps; just keep telling yourself you can do it and make yourself stronger.

As an orange belt, one can start taking sparring classes on Friday night. This was always a little intimidating for me because you sometimes were matched up with higher ranks that could literally take you down in two seconds! However, the black belts are taught to push the lower ranks. They need to know what their skills are and control their powerful punches and kicks and not make full contact to the head. Well, it was my third sparring night and I was matched with a very good young male black belt. I believe he was around 14 years old. I thought I was doing well until I spun around and fell to the ground. He had thrown a spinning wheel kick and swiped it right into the side of my face across my eye. I didn't feel pain but I wasn't sure what had happened.

The master at the dojo took me off the mats and sat me down. They gave me ice and immediately called my husband. Of course this happened on one of the few nights that he was not there. I remember the owner of the school was also there and I heard him say, "Is that just her makeup that got smeared around her eye?" They told me to put the ice on my eye but not to look in the mirror. My husband came and we looked at my eyes. It was not just my makeup; I had some bruising which started immediately and a nice cut across the top of my eyelid. We went to the Emergency Room where they asked questions about what happened. I made sure they knew it was from karate as everyone was looking at my husband funny. X-rays and a CT of my face were done to make sure no fractures of the bones had occurred. Everything was negative, I just needed a couple of stitches on my eyelid. The nurse came with the needle and I remember my younger son thought it was so cool and watched her stitch up my eye while my older son did not want to watch any of it. The whole family was there now because the boys at the time were too young to be home alone. So I had stitches for a week and thankfully my long hair, or sunglasses, could cover my eye. It's amazing the first thing people think of when they see a woman with a black eye. I had to explain to coworkers and my patients at work what had happened. Many of them said there was no way they could do sparring class or karate at all. There is always a chance you can get hurt no matter what rank you are.

After my sparring accident, it took me a couple weeks to heal. Was I afraid to spar again? Of course I was. I did not give up though. I kept going and making myself better. I learned from this accident that you should always have control of your actions. The gentleman I was sparring with was an incredible fighter and very POWERFUL. However, he should have realized he was sparring a lower rank and not have thrown such an advanced technique wildly. You can push others to learn but not always show that you can beat everyone. Sometimes people need to learn to take it down a notch and not be so much of a showoff in their skills depending on who they are fighting, especially lower ranks. I later learned that this individual had a tendency to lose control of his techniques in several encounters with different people. It taught me to be in control on the mats especially when teaching someone who is a lower rank or may be more timid and less aggressive. One should always be aware of their surroundings and the abilities of the other students. Friday night, sparring night, became fun again when eventually our whole family would be there sometimes sparring with each other. The instructors would match us up together and it was always fun when it was mother against son or son against father. My two sons soon were very good and thought they were stronger than their mother.

Soon I was training with my younger son, to receive our black belts. The black belt test was the most physical test I have ever taken. Mentally and physically, it challenged me and pushed me to limits I thought never possible. Being on the mats with all the masters checking out your technique was terrifying, but as I started the test I got so excited and really zoned in on what I had been training for. At the very end of the test was sparring and that took everything I had left to complete my test. My son too pushed himself. While I was testing, he too was going through his drills and almost passed out. He was given some water and then continued to pass the different stations of testing. In the end, it was an awesome feeling to know that I had passed this level with my youngest son. The whole family had received our black belts and were the first family to do so at our dojo.

I enjoyed going to black belt class and learning more advanced techniques and self-defense. However, as life goes on sometimes it is challenging to get to class. My younger son has had an interest in trying sports in school, wrestling, and track, which takes time away from the dojo. My older son, now a senior in high school, had started marching band, which took most of his time in the fall. He also started working at a local grocery store in the evening and became more interested in going to the gym than karate. I have also become busy with other activities but have never given up my kickboxing class which is what I originally started with.

Throughout life, many things come and go, but karate and martial arts remain forever. One can always go back to the dojo and depending on your level continue to learn and improve yourself or help someone else. Although my boys have grown and maybe at the time have other interests or activities, martial arts will always be a part of their growing up and will remain part of them forever. Martial arts remain something they can always be a part of and return to in the future. For me, the dojo is somewhere I can always return. At times in life, other adventures and family responsibilities take time away from training, but the martial arts is part of you, not only on the mats but in the way you treat each other with respect and kindness. In the future, possibilities are open to teach classes at the dojo or just help out when needed.

Advice and tips:

1. Follow what inspires you in class and on the dojo. If training gets hard, focus on the things you truly enjoy about karate.

2. All instructors teach differently, don't allow the one you may not prefer to bring you down, always believe in yourself and move on.

3. Sometimes when you feel you have no time, go to class, it will help you step away from life and refocus on yourself creating less stress.

4. Create bonds with your children and fun memories during karate classes.

5. Try sparring, it will be intimidating at first, but it's fun and makes you stronger and helps you use mushin, no mind just throwing whatever techniques come to your mind.

6. Take classes as a family; it truly is a memory I will always have and it was so great to be all on the mats together.

7. If you have an interest, follow a Sensei you look up to and learn the skill to teach others.

8. Never give up on yourself

9. Ask people to help you learn something you have difficulty with.

Nathalie Mackerer

Becoming a mother has made me next-level confident. I've never felt more empowered.

Kelly Clarkson

You Never Know

I had no desire to ever do martial arts when I was younger. It was not anything I really knew about, but here I am now, 55 years old and a 4th-degree black belt in Kenpo karate. My path here was winding, but I am here and still going! It started something like this…

Around 34 or 35 years old, a mom of two young kids was asked by a neighbor to start going to a yoga studio in the area. It was fine for a year, but the owners' actual backgrounds were in kickboxing, Muay Thai, and BJJ, so we started to learn these techniques in a women's morning boot camp. After a while, the instructor, Shelley, asked us if we wanted to go see an MMA fight and we did. I was fascinated and wanted to get more involved, however, I was a mother of two kids. I was not going to be doing any MMA fights anytime soon. Still, I got involved enough to meet people and make friends in this setting.

At the same time, my son's friend was doing karate and asked him to do it. So, my son Alex started it around 4th grade. I would bring him to class and the instructor was very nice, techniques were practical and easy to follow. Finally, Darryl Hinthorne, the owner/instructor of Kenpo Martial Arts

Centers said to me why don't I try it. When the boot camp had to close, I did!

I am not a gym person, so I was not interested in going to a gym, but after having two young kids, I knew I needed to do something to get in shape. So, I started going to karate classes. They were fun and I was learning self-defense techniques that did not feel like work.

I started as a white belt learning new movements, then I learned combinations and Kenpo movements, getting a new colored belt every few months. I kept going and thinking I would never reach black belt. I was never coordinated in sports but with karate, I decided it was all about me and progressing, to get better. I was addicted and wanted to go to class instead of other stuff.

With perseverance, I was going to stick to this and do better. It helped me become determined to progress myself. When sparring was no longer about trying to win but learning how to block a punch and give one back, I loved it! During that time, I missed some kid events, stopped going to PTO meetings, and was not exactly doing the usual stuff moms do. I am still feeling like I should have gone to a women's boot camp or yoga class, but that was not me.

In the beginning, both kids were going to class and it was great to go with them. Then my daughter stopped and school/homework got to be too much for my son, so he had to stop too. I kept going and reached black belt.

I started karate in 2006 at age 38. I got my black belt at age 44 in 2012. Then, I wanted Alex to come back and continue. He had stopped just below brown belt so he needed to continue to get to black belt. This was one thing I could share with my son to keep doing. In June of 2022, I did my 4th-degree test with his 1st-degree test!! It was awesome!! Alex does not go as much, but I do get him there at least once a week. It is our connection!

My perseverance in continuing has gotten me to 4th degree black belt and I am there all the time, learning, and helping teach. Time practicing got me through the COVID years when there was not much else to do, but our school was open for private lessons.

I am the highest female in our small school. To most, that does not mean much, but to me, it is because of family support, my husband being ok with me going to class most nights and not being home to do the typical mother stuff, kids being ok with me balancing my stuff with when they needed me. Also helping was the encouragement of all the guys in class for me to keep going. I have made many friends in this world that I would not have if not for martial arts lessons and going to various seminars.

Now, here's the hard part I have found about being female, a wife, and a mom interested in martial arts. It is hard to sometimes justify to my family that mom is leaving them for a seminar or class to learn how to fight and use weapons. I sometimes would prefer to go to these things as opposed to things with them. A family vacation is happening during the weekend of a loved symposium that now I cannot go to because of the need for family time. I feel like it is probably easier for our male counterparts to take off for a seminar without doing all the juggling we need to do to go to these things. My life has had a lot of juggling with the balance between being a wife and taking care of two kids (at least they are now 26 and 23), but also recently helping to care for my mother with ALS, seven hours away, involving several weekends this past year. Fitting in my martial arts classes and learning was a balancing act of just the basics. There was no extra learning. Things should slow down now, and I will be able to work on my needs and desire to learn in this martial arts world.

Overall, I am thrilled with my choice to take karate and be involved with martial arts. I call it my greatest skill I hope to never use, but I know I have used it. It has helped with my awareness of things around me, it has built confidence in being able to talk to all kinds of people in my job as a home physical therapist, and it has allowed me a sense of security in knowing some things when I have been walking in neighborhoods and going into people's houses. I have traveled on mission trips to various countries for physical therapy and felt good enough about my knowledge to do a week-long kids' karate class while in Guatemala!

I have been doing this for 18 years now. My family knows that if they cannot find me at home, I am at karate. I call it my second home. I am trying to help Kenpo Martial Arts thrive. I am learning how to teach, be around kids, and work with adults. I do love it when little girls show up at the school, and I hope that they see me and have some inspiration that they can go far in this, that it is not just a boy's thing. We need more women in the room to have a presence and we need this too. We are learning skills that are in reality brutal but disguised for fun. They will be useful someday, but I hope not!

Cara Crisafulli

If I were asked to define Motherhood, I would have defined it as Love in its purest form. Unconditional Love.

Revathi Sankaran

Martial Arts (Grand)Mom

The story of my martial arts journey began similar to that of
other moms at my school: my child started training first. By
the time my daughter became an advanced colored belt in
Taekwondo, I had been observing for a while and that's when
she attempted to convince me that I should train too. I was
both hesitant and skeptical. Watching my daughter's belt
tests, I was in awe each time I saw the students perform their
patterns in harmony. By then, my daughter was only a few
months away from testing for Black Belt and the thought of
sharing time on the mats with her was intriguing. I was
reasonably fit from mountain climbing and running, and had
dabbled in some kickboxing classes, so it wasn't the sheer
amount of physical activity that I found intimidating. Rather,
I had previously taken a short series of self-defense classes at
my workplace, taught by her Taekwondo instructor. I had
tremendous difficulty sequencing movements during line
drills and I lacked the body awareness to properly execute
individual techniques. How would I ever manage to learn
"forms"? It seemed beyond my capabilities. Despite my
misgivings and after months of coaxing, I eventually had the
courage to enroll in Taekwondo.

I'm guessing that some of what I've written so far resonates
with other moms: the child beginning their training in martial

arts first, then the parent joining in after watching from the sidelines. The self-doubt might also sound familiar to others, though the cause might stem more from the anticipated physical demands than the mental ones that nearly prevented me from practicing martial arts. So, here's where my story deviates from others – my daughter wasn't in pre-school or elementary school when she began Taekwondo. She wasn't in middle school either, or even in high school. She was a college student and I was in my mid-fifties!

I recall vividly when I was first aware that my daughter had begun training in Taekwondo. At the time, she was enrolled in a college nearby and lived close to home. We were standing outside and she wanted to show me something in the trunk of her car. It was the sparring gear she'd just ordered! I clearly had no understanding or appreciation of what it meant to her. That's when she told me about the martial arts classes she was taking and how it had been a long-time dream of hers. She'd done her research and chosen the dojang herself, and she was paying for her own classes. I witnessed her excitement but was still clueless. It wasn't until months later, when she told me about an upcoming belt test, that I ever observed her at the school. After watching her advance through several more ranks, she said, "Mom, you should do this too. I think you'd really like it."

Besides the trepidation in learning Taekwondo forms, there were other practical considerations in my decision-making process. First, enrollment in any martial arts program entails a financial commitment. As a mom of three children (two in college at the time), I was used to spending money for our family and for their activities but had never budgeted any significant amount for myself. That was common in my parents' generation, probably less so in my own. After so

many years of financial sacrifices on behalf of my children, I
would have to spend money on myself; I needed to be okay
with allocating funds for myself, a level of spending that
involved signing an annual contract. Ultimately, I determined
that my needs were important, and that "I was worth it." If I
wanted to be a role model for my children, I had to show
them how to value themselves and I could only do that by
valuing myself and my place in our family.

A second factor, and as significant as the financial
component, would be the time commitment required for
participating in martial arts. Classes were offered four nights
each week and twice in the daytime. For the adult program in
which I enrolled, I was encouraged to attend three classes per
week, not counting specialty classes like forms review,
weapons, and self-defense. Including travel time and time for
changing, that would mean two-and-a-half to three hours
spent for an evening class. It meant that I wouldn't be
present to either prepare or eat dinner with the rest of the
family. Even though I didn't have young children that
required my attention, I wouldn't be available on evenings
that I attended class.

Finally, there was one other important consideration: I would
be the oldest student at the school. Unlike some other
parents, I had no prior experience in martial arts from my
youth and no muscle memory on which to rely. My age
meant that my flexibility was reduced and my joints were
more likely to ache. I couldn't run as fast or jump as high as
my younger self and certainly would not be able to match the
skills of the teens at the school. My body required more
recovery time and I'd have to dance the line between pushing
my limits and overdoing. Fortunately, the wisdom that
comes with age more than compensated for the natural

decrease in performance and it did not prevent me from becoming a martial artist.

Although my decision to train in Taekwondo wasn't automatic, requiring months of serious discernment, it was one of the best decisions I've made. I can't imagine my life without martial arts. Obviously, for anyone who has succeeded in becoming a Black Belt, especially a mom, the sacrifices are real but they pale in comparison to the rewards. I may have initiated my training at my daughter's urging and as a way of spending time with her, but it soon became my own passion. As I progressed through the colored belt ranks, I saw her achieve her First and Second Dan. By my fourth year though, she had paused her training. It was disappointing that she wasn't able to be on the mats with me as I prepared for my first Black Belt test, but it reinforced the concept that the journey was my own. In fact, the personal form I created for that test was in the shape of an infinity symbol: the left side included techniques I learned while my daughter and I trained together, and the right side represented a combination of techniques I had learned on my own. Alongside my husband and her younger sibling, our daughter was there with her husband on the day of my test, cheering me on while holding their two-week-old son. That newborn was my first grandchild, making me a Black Belt Grandmom!

Since becoming a Black Belt, I qualified to share judging responsibilities with my daughter at colored belt tests. Once again, she was there to take the lead. I continued my training and went on to receive my Second and Third Dan. My daughter had a second child and although she has since put her training on hold, our common experience in Taekwondo gives us a special mother-daughter bond.

My parting advice to other moms is to squelch whatever fears
and doubts might prevent you from becoming a martial artist.
Sharing the experience with other family members will
broaden and deepen your relationships. The sacrifices are
worth it and the rewards are real!

Denise McQuade

*Such a mysterious business,
motherhood. How brave a woman
must be to embark on it.*

M. L. Stedman

Participation Medal leads to Participation

I knew it was coming, his father knew it was coming. His instructors knew, even his peers. The only one surprised was him.

What was harder? Seeing his face, shoulders, body droop or knowing I'd have to pick up the pieces?

I walked down to the floor and slowly off to the side of the ring where the other parents were standing. As he saw me and started making his way through the crowd, I put on a big smile. I wrapped him in a warm hug and congratulated him on his form.

"Mom, I don't understand," he whispered into my shoulder.

"You did great," I said as I squeezed him tighter.

As he pulled out of my embrace he asked a flurry of questions. Was the score an error, did they not flip the right number card over on the score plaque, did I see the three original numbers, did they remember to add all three up and then divide?

"No, there was no error, let's go sit down." I took his hand and guided him to a quieter spot in the loud gymnasium.

"I quit. I'm done. I don't want this belt," he huffed as he struggled to undo the knot. He tossed his belt to the side and sat down across from me.

I sighed. Four and a half years. What was I supposed to do? Pull him in for another hug, tell him it's OK, let's go home and call it a day? He'd love that. Heck, I'd love that. Easier for everyone. I could hear my inner voice, which always seemed to sound like my father, "You know you can't always take the easy way out."

"Nope, not an option" I said before I let that easy way try to sneak in again.

He glared at me. He was mad. And probably embarrassed, ashamed, and disappointed. I felt a few of those emotions as well. I tried to trust that inner voice; it didn't usually steer me wrong. Four and a half years. One participation medal couldn't throw that out the window.

"I think I see why the scoring went the way it did, would you like to talk about it?" His stare was icy, but I waited for a response.

"I suck!" Now my shoulders took their turn and drooped. That word. Suck. He had always lacked confidence, especially in sports, but I still hated to hear him say it.

"You do not suck," I said firmly. And I believed it. "But would it be fair to say that that was not your best performance?" He nodded, so I pushed on. "Practicing, how much did you do before today?"

As he started to argue that he did a lot, the words trailed off. We both knew it wasn't enough. Not even close.

I started to blame myself. I should have pushed him more, should have brought him to more classes. I should have enforced nightly practices, requested a private lesson at the dojo.

No. Hard stop. This was a positive conversation. To him and to myself.

I took a deep breath and went for a different approach. "What were the goals you had for today?"

"I wanted first place… That didn't happen," his attitude dripped off the comment.

"Nope, not this time," I said with an upbeat tone. I followed his eyes to the first-place winner. "How do you think he got there?"

"Practice." He rolled his eyes, hard.

There was my opening. Humor. I have always been able to reach this kid with humor. "You roll your eyes like a pro. You're nine and you roll them like a teenager. Let's get your safety rolls to be as smooth as your eye rolls."

"Mommmmmmmmmm" he moaned as they rolled again.

Victory. I felt the conversation turn. "Oh, come on, that was funny!"

"Ya," he admitted as a smile crept up his face.

"OK. Grab your belt, we can try again," I said and started to stand up. My mind moved as I did. He wasn't quitting martial arts, we'd talk in the car about how to move forward, how to hit the goals he had.

"We?" He grabbed my hand and pulled me back down. He zeroed in on that word. That one little word.

His eyes pleaded as he waited for my response. Just as I knew humor would win him, he knew his eyes would win me. "We. Mom, you said we. We means us right? Are you going to start again? Are you going to compete with me?"

I was a yellow belt, but I hadn't been to classes in months. Hadn't been working out, practicing, or anything. I'd been holding down two jobs, two kids, one husband, and a house. I'd been a personal chef, maid, and chauffeur, not a martial artist.

My mind began to race. Compete? I simply meant I would help him prepare for the next tournament. I would help set him up for success, make him practice, bring him to more classes, have him lock in that form. I didn't mean I'd be safety rolling on a gymnasium floor in front of 300 people.

I realized he was still talking. "We could practice outside, there's more room and the weather is getting nicer. I could show you the form I'm working on, because your form is just a beginner form and isn't really great for tournaments. Oh man, will the next tournament have synchronized forms?!"

I took a breath. And then another one. He moved fast. But he had also gone from quitting martial arts to brainstorming the next tournament in three minutes flat. That was impressive. That turnaround deserved something.

"Would me starting up again help you with your goals?"

"YUP!" He was now standing over me, beaming from ear to ear.

His smile filled me with excitement. It was contagious. I looked up at him and said "OK. Let's get me up, I can't be sitting on a wooden floor for hours if I'm going to be in class tomorrow."

He pulled me up and into one last embrace before he ran over to the stands where our dojo had set up for the day.

I picked up his belt and began making my way behind him. There was the victory. That conversation had turned, not the way that I had thought it would, but ultimately into a way that was going to benefit us both. I had wanted to get back to classes but had solidly stationed myself on the back burner while making sure others' needs were met. That boy had figured out how to satisfy my desire to put him first while at the same time having me pick back up a sport that I so enjoyed. Again, impressive.

Motherhood is hard. There is an unspoken rule that children come first, and mothers come second. Meet their needs, fulfill their hopes and dreams, and help them succeed. Then, if you have time, do it all again, for yourself. But there is another rule, one known by any air traveler. If the oxygen masks drop, secure yours before helping others. You aren't good to anyone if you are unconscious.

I find it hard to follow both rules. Sometimes I need a bridge. Restarting martial arts to help my son is the self-care I need and almost more importantly, deserve. By practicing at home with him and running through forms, we are preparing for that tournament first-place trophy, his goal. For myself, I am carving out time for classes and going with my mind solely focused on the material, not on other responsibilities. Allowing myself to identify as me, and not just mother and wife.

Self-care can come in many forms, all of which are valid and belong on the front burner, but I find that martial arts check off more boxes than the average activity. For me, they provide such an immersive experience that it helps my brain quiet down and push past the bills to be paid, the emails to be answered, and the grocery shopping to be completed. They also double as a workout, taking the need to hit the gym out of the equation. Martial arts work my mind, my body, and my spirit. All of which, when satisfied, make me a better mother, more refreshed, and ready for the next thing.

Someday I will follow both rules without a bridge, without the need to verbally qualify that both are happening. Until then, I will be gentle with myself and my child, reminding both of us that this is hard and we are only human.

Alisson Donnelly

"You have suffered enough." That became my mantra for motherhood from there on out. You have suffered enough. If you can make it easier, make it easier, and don't feel guilty about it.

Ali Wong

Modern TKD Mom

My name is Sylvie Henley, and I am a martial arts mom! I came to martial arts through my son at four or five years old. We wanted him to do an activity on Saturday mornings. He was invited to a class during "bring-a-friend week" by my niece at our local taekwondo school. It was a big hit at first. He did it for about six months and then his interest started to waver. I offered to join him in class hoping to get him to keep going a little while longer. It worked for a while. Altogether, I think he lasted two years.

One of the challenges I had in those early years was balancing being a mom and a student at the same time. Our classes are generally all mixed. My son and I were in the same beginner class. It was tough to navigate how to gently encourage him, but not discipline him in class. Our instructor always made it very clear that when we were in class, he was under her authority and I was a student, not mom. Looking back now, it really was a gift for both of us. It taught him the discipline and respect he needed to follow directions, and me the opportunity to grow and learn.

The athlete and perfectionist in me quickly latched onto taekwondo. I loved having a new skill to learn and work on.

I had done sports before, but everything felt awkward. The movements were so unfamiliar to me, they didn't make sense. But I enjoyed trying to understand them. It was a blessing for me to finally have a slice of life that was just for me. I wasn't "mom" in class, or an employee, or a wife. I was a student learning alongside everyone else. It was a great escape from all the other things vying for my attention. Taekwondo gave me something to focus on just for my own self-improvement.

One of the challenges I faced, was that as I got more into my training, my son got less into it. I got moved out of the beginner class and that made it really hard to figure out what to do with him while I was in the next class. We used to bring in a laptop that would play movies. That worked for a while until the DVD player component started acting up and wouldn't work. Then he got bored and wanted to go. Then I asked if any of the other local moms in the beginner class would be willing to host a short play date with him while I attended my class. We did that twice. It wasn't a long enough time for him to really settle in and play with the other child. It was really frustrating for both of us for a while. We finally decided that he is more of a soccer player than a martial artist. I couldn't do the arguing to practice or time to go to class anymore. He didn't do that with soccer. So, we let him stop. It was clear soccer was his preference. I was sad not to do something with him, but the blessing was that it allowed me to concentrate on myself.

One of the biggest benefits of doing martial arts was the community of other women I found there. Our school is fortunate enough to be 50% women. I found a group of women who welcomed me into their circle and showed me how to practice forms on my own. It didn't make sense to me until I started doing forms with them outside of class. All of a sudden, it started making sense. We built a good community of support. It was nice to have other mom friends outside of work in taekwondo class. That friendship was one of the reasons I kept coming back. I wanted to be there with them and train with them. It was fun! I really needed that in my life.

Each time I go to class, I find I make a choice to be there. Some days it's out of commitment, sometimes it's for my mental health, and others I just need to blow off steam through physical activity. Each time I come, I need to leave the outside world behind and be fully present. Sometimes I just need to be in class for me, where I'm not giving pieces of myself to others.

Balancing home, work, and class is a hard challenge that each of us navigates differently. Everyone's journey is different. Often, it is not a straight path. There are many detours and delays that can happen along the way. Be sure to give yourself grace. It's not a race. Commit to being a life-long learner. Be curious and ask questions. Take the time to make friends.

One of the characteristics that I've noticed since doing martial arts, is that I am a lot more resilient than I used to be. Getting up after a fall, changing directions on the spot, facing new challenges, and navigating relationships has made me stronger. I'm not the same person that I was when I first started. I'm stronger than I was.

I've also learned a lot about myself along the way. I am an introvert by nature. I don't like change and being put on the spot. I still get nervous in front of a class. I like to plan, know things ahead of time, and be able to process new information. Being in martial arts has certainly gotten me out of my comfort zone. I've had to do all of those things on short notice. I have learned to think and do more "on the fly". I have also found that my style of teaching is much more one-on-one mentoring. I like to teach the tricks that helped me learn and build a good teacher/student relationship that way. I'm different that way, and that's ok. Each one of us is unique and adds to martial arts. We all have something to contribute. We are stronger together! Modern Moms of Martial Arts, let's do this and make this world a better place!

Sylvie Henley

*There's no way to be a perfect mother
and a million ways to be a good one.*

Jill Churchill

"It's About Being Your Best"

When I was a teenager, training multiple days a week at my karate dojo, I began to dream of opening my own school someday. The dream was there, although I never really pictured what it would look like – I just knew I wanted to teach martial arts, and I definitely wanted my school to be a safe space for kids to train. Our dojo was great, however, it was not the most inviting environment for young kids. They were welcome to try a few classes out, but it was pretty clear none of the instructors enjoyed teaching little ones.

My life between that season and the one when my husband and I actually opened our own martial arts school ended up quite adventurous – I spent multiple years living in places where my martial arts training was applied in very practical ways. I was incredibly grateful for the training I'd received, and the ways it contributed to keeping me safe and alert.

One of the things I never thought of was the physical toll life as a missionary in a rural orphanage would take on me, and by the time we opened our school, my body wasn't even close to competitive shape anymore. I struggled with that – how could I teach people things I physically couldn't do myself? I had a messed up back, hip, feet, wrist, the list went on.

As we discussed opening a dojo, I really hesitated. Not because I didn't want to – I was so very excited to teach others what had literally saved my life and was one of the happiest experiences of my own childhood.

It was because of this nagging thought in the back of my mind – *I'm not good enough*. Not because I didn't know the particular techniques or applications, but because I was now much more physically limited than I had ever been before.

It's a double-edged sword, being a martial artist. Arguably, physical fitness is really a crucial piece. You can't engage in an intense physical activity without being able to engage in such, right?

When I began my martial arts journey, I had a great team of instructors, and I am so thankful for each of them. They took the eager twelve-year-old kid I was and pushed me to learn and grow in ways I was yearning to. They taught me skills, both on and off the mats, that were valuable for all of life.

However – they also taught me a few things I had to unlearn. I do not discredit my instructors in any way, but as we grow and learn and develop a deeper understanding of the things we have been taught over the years, we (hopefully) filter them through the lens of greater understanding.

One element of my training that I had to unlearn was the very thing I came up against as we prepared to open our school – that unless you are physically fit, you can't teach.

It took time to learn that I didn't have to do everything in order to be a good teacher. I could teach my students wrist locks even if I didn't have the grip strength to perform one on my right side. I could teach them kicks even though my heel hurt too bad to support me while performing more than a few of those kicks.

My students were learning, and performing well, in spite of my inadequacies – but I still had those memories in the back of my mind that haunted me.

A sharp memory was when a lady who wanted to test for black belt was told a firm 'absolutely not going to happen' by my sensei because she had needed a hip replacement and taken six months off from training. She came in after having been gone, wanting to discuss getting back into shape, and, for reasons unknown to me, he was very clear that her training days were over.

It scared me that day – I realized that I was one injury away from being disqualified from my dreams.

I don't blame my sensei, nor any of the other instructors whose go-to response to any sort of expressed pain was 'suck it up, Buttercup'. I heard all of the quotes over the years – and believed them.

Pain is weakness leaving the body.

No pain, no gain.

I remember breaking a toe one day in the dojo, and being told, "You have nine good ones, stop complaining".

I would assume that we've all seen *The Karate Kid*. While most of us agree John Kreese was a jerk who took things too far, there's the element of 'this is what a karate dojo is like' that we subconsciously accept.

I did. Though my instructors were not cruel, and they took great care of us when we truly were injured – there was always the drive to be tougher, complain less, and ignore pain. For me it was compounded by the nagging fear that 'this injury might mean I'm done', and therefore the internal push to pretend it didn't hurt as bad as it did.

Being one of the few girls training amongst boys and men, I felt that pressure even harder – although I honestly cannot say whether it was a stronger pressure from within or without. I wanted to keep up with the guys – to be the 'last man standing' in all the challenges they threw at our class. And often, I was. I kept up, ignored pain, pushed myself, and was quite proud of the martial artist I became.

And, over the years, my body began to break down – more rapidly than I had expected, because of the adventures I'd lived through.

I struggled with that. When we first started our school I felt incredibly inadequate as a teacher. My body had just gone through a really rough pregnancy, on top of my previous issues and old injuries. I was getting up multiple times in the night with my little one, as do all mamas in the world. I coordinated classes to work with naptimes and trips to grandma's house when my kiddos were really little, and, as they got older, I worked out class schedules to make sure only people they felt safe around would be waiting in our living room when they were home. It was an added challenge, but one that was vitally important.

And all along, I was watching my students grow and thrive. I felt incredibly subconscious about my physical limitations – and also frustrated because the new aches and pains weren't the kind I could just 'push through' – they were legitimately stopping me from action.

It was confusing – because we were doing exactly what I'd always dreamed of doing, and creating an environment where everyone was welcome – the clumsiest kid and the most polished athlete were equally welcome and treated the same in our classes. I would watch my students struggle and come up with creative solutions, all the while still feeling as though I myself shouldn't be teaching.

As I worked through teaching the things I was passionate about and knew on the inside that I couldn't perform on the outside, I grew as a person. I learned how to communicate more clearly and demonstrate things in new ways because the ways I had been taught didn't work for my body anymore. I had the best students (I'm sure all of us say that, as well we should), and they learned and grew as I did.

One of the surprising elements was that being a mom taught me so much about being a good sensei! My family means more to me than anything else on this earth – my three kiddos are incredible people and some of my very closest friends.

Having my own two daughters and son in my classes has been an incredible learning experience. I know them – I know their personalities and am very aware that what can be incredibly challenging to one of my daughters is a total breeze to my other one. My oldest is one of those with quiet strength in the dojo. She doesn't seek the spotlight, and she's not the type to volunteer or jump in first when we start a drill or sparring matches. But she gets in there and shocks people with how well she can hold her own. I love that about my girl.

My other daughter is the passionate one with all the ideas and all the energy. She often misses the details when we're explaining a drill because she's so eager to jump in and do it, but she throws her heart and soul into every single thing she does. I love her eagerness and passion, and she is also quite a force to be reckoned with.

My son is cautious. He loves karate, but he is an astute observer who wants lots of time to process what's expected of him before he jumps in and tries it. At times people consider him shy – but he's just working out how he feels about different situations. I love that he is so wise, even though he's only in second grade.

Knowing them makes teaching them easier. I can anticipate what will be challenging and prepare accordingly. We do hard things – but we process and grow through them together.

As I have worked with my littles, both homeschooling them and having them as students in the dojo, I've learned that we can face hard things head-on, together, and we don't have to do it the way my dojo did. My kids don't have to fear being 'disqualified' when they fail. One of our very favorite things to say (the theme of our homeschool) is, "Mistakes are proof you are trying." As long as you're trying, you're learning and growing. I love that we've been able to cultivate that environment.

I remember being at a tournament when my oldest had just turned eight. She was terrified of doing her form in front of judges and cried because the thought of performing while they watched was terrifying to her. When they called her name, she got up, stumbled through a small portion, and then awkwardly bowed and rushed off, collapsing into tears on the sidelines. By all accounts she had failed – but I remember hugging her and choosing to point out the positive – she hadn't even wanted to step foot in that ring, and she'd been brave enough to do it! I really was proud of her, because that was about the hardest thing you could have asked of my girl at that time.

The funny thing is, those judges wrote her off as another unprepared white belt – and from their point of view, she was. But that experience helped her. A few minutes later, in her flag sparring division, she took third place out of about fifteen kids, and one of the judges commented, "Wow, she's tougher than I thought!"

And then she got in there and sparred. During her second match, a kid kicked her right in the face. There was blood everywhere, they had to shut down the ring and sanitize everything, and it took her nose a few minutes to stop bleeding.

When her tears stopped, she looked at me with a twinkle in her eye and said, "I'm okay, Mom, I wanna keep going."

And she did. I couldn't care less if she won or lost the next match – that day was absolutely a huge win for my little girl. She overcame. Nobody talked about what place she won – that wasn't important. She took on her fears in so many different ways and came out the victor.

I tell that story because I am so very proud and thankful for the beautiful ways my kiddos have grown as people through martial arts – and because of them, I have grown both as a mom and a martial artist.

Perhaps the most poignant lesson I learned, and one that has been reinforced as I watch my kids grow and adapt, was that the things I *couldn't* physically do left room for me to grow and excel even more at the things I *could* do. One of the beautiful pieces of this development of understanding was that, as I studied martial arts history, I realized we really come from a line of adapters – not super-humans.

The karate I was taught was rigid, unchanging, and unyielding. There was some comfort in that – but it didn't leave much room for adaptation.

One instructor was a brave soul – he was the only one who would challenge me to do things differently if they didn't work, in the context of self-defense. Those lessons in adaptation literally saved my life – and greatly influenced my own development of curriculum.

Adaptation – the ability to grow in the context in which you live, is one of the greatest skills you can develop.

When I was pregnant with my son, I would have to sit down while running sparring matches, but I learned that I can teach just as effectively sitting in a chair – it's just not as much fun. But I adapted.

I grew stronger – because I can't do certain things, I became better at doing others. And as the years have gone by, I realize how much I've grown as a teacher. Where I used to fear holding my students back by not being able to perform all that I ask of them, I now have come to realize that I'm actually giving them perspective as they learn. It's the same with my own kiddos – there were things I did growing up that my own kids will never do, and things they are doing that I never could have dreamed of! The natural response, I think, is to resist and fear change. We are creatures of habit, and it is so easy for us to think that because we've always done something a certain way, it is the only way that thing can be done – isn't it?

In life as a mom it's a joy to watch my kids try new things, be passionate about subjects I never would have even thought of, and have the courage to do hard things. I didn't stop my son from trying to climb the play structure in pursuit of his sisters because I knew he was too small – I let him try, and try again, until he finally figured out that, though he may not be able to scramble up like they did, he could work his way up a different way.

Years ago I heard *encouragement* explained as 'giving someone courage'. By cheering them on, you're literally building their courage. It's one of the core things that makes our martial arts school special – we push encouragement as one of the most important elements.

And by focusing on encouragement, it really helps in all areas of life. My instructors back when I was a teen were encouraging – as long as I was winning or excelling.

They were wonderful – but this time around, our students get encouragement from us no matter how things go. If they tried their hardest, it doesn't matter if they won. If they pushed themselves to do their best in that situation, then the outcome of 'win or lose' isn't important.

In class we have had all types of students, and I absolutely love that. As long as you're willing to learn and have a good attitude, you're welcome – regardless of your physical capabilities.

The fun part? It's not about being the best. It's about being *your* best. I can be a confident martial arts instructor even though my body doesn't do all the things I would love for it to.

I can be a good mom even though I will never be good at the things my kids are good at. That's not the point. I never expected such from others – it just took me a while to learn it about myself.

If I could give some 'mom advice' to my fellow mamas out there – remember how critically important your encouragement is to your kids. It's not about being the best, it's about being better than you were yesterday. If you hear a critical inner voice telling you that you aren't good enough, or you can't do something, take it into consideration, but don't let it hold you back. You may actually not be able to perform a certain technique. That doesn't mean you fail as a martial artist. Your kids may not be able to do all of the things you want them to – but make sure your definition of success is confident, happy kids, even if they aren't as 'good' as you want them to be at certain things. They need your encouragement, and you will all grow more personally than you ever thought possible by focusing on the positive.

Jenni Siu

*Motherhood:
all love begins and ends there.*

Robert Browning

From Cars to Karate

At some point, people stopped asking me what was next for
me or what I wanted to do with the rest of my life. I don't
know when exactly this happened, probably around the same
time I started to be called "ma'am" instead of "miss", and
around the time I left my career to be a stay-at-home mom. I
am not blameless in this. I allowed my life, once full of
meaningful work, slightly less meaningful meetings, and social
obligations, to be replaced with feeding schedules doctor's
appointments, and late-night diaper runs. Somewhere
between the endless laps around the living room trying to
convince a small human to sleep and watching the movie *Cars*
for the 25th time, my world got very small. The larger outside
world was different now and I did not seem to be a part of it.
People were talking about current events and new songs on
the radio and that amazing season finale of the show I used
to watch, but the only thing I was listening to was the *Cars*
soundtrack on repeat, and the only thing I could think of to
start a conversation with was an observation about Lightning
McQueen's story arc or the nuances of Mater. *Cars* is really a
great movie, though.

My family always made me feel needed of course, but the rest
of the world saw me as a redundant figure. I found that more

often than not, when having a casual conversation with someone, the first and only question I was asked was, "How are the kids?" I was no longer an individual with my own interests and insights. Or at least that's what it seemed like to me, although I wasn't doing much to prove them wrong, either. I wasn't advertising my new adventures away from motherhood because I wasn't really having any. There were opportunities for me to reengage with the world beyond my home and family, but I never took advantage of them. My attitude towards the various possibilities of starting something new ranged from unsure of myself to terrified. I'd been in mom mode for so long, I didn't have the confidence to step out of it. So in all fairness, while no one asked me what my plans were for the future, I didn't have any anyway.

Then something unexpected happened: my children showed an interest in taking Karate. A Karate instructor had come to their school and done a demonstration in their PE classes, and both of them were immediately hooked. I could not have been more supportive of this and immediately went to work contacting the dojo and signing them up. I had desperately wanted to take martial arts classes as a child but never had the chance. I was told there weren't any classes offered around us, although conveniently there was a dance studio; after a few recitals of me being (appropriately) placed in the back left corner of the stage during the performance, it was decided I should leave dance behind. Since I didn't have a talent for dance, in my mind I decided I would have failed at martial arts as well and the idea was never visited again. Now my children were taking martial arts and excelling in it. I was so excited for them, and surprisingly for myself as well. I looked forward to them showing me what they learned in class - how to make a proper fist, how to do a proper takedown, what a "form" was. I loved learning from them and with them. But it never crossed my mind to take classes myself. My chance had passed.

I knew there was an adult program at the dojo. The instructors had approached me a few times and encouraged me to take a class or two, but I had all the ready-made excuses not to partake: I was too busy, my family needed me to be home in the evenings, I'm not up for it, I'm too old. Thankfully the instructors persisted and as a result of their patience, I began to believe that taking martial arts classes was something I could possibly do, albeit nervously.

My involvement in martial arts happened very slowly: I took a four-week women's self-defense course, then a free one-month trial complete with uniform, and next a combined parent/child class to get me more involved. With each class, each belt progression, and each tournament I attended, my world got bigger and my confidence grew. I began leaving my comfort zone a lot more often and became more comfortable in doing so. I discovered newfound resilience, but I also learned to be kind to myself when I experienced defeat. My kids were also benefiting from my martial arts journey. They were seeing how important it was to never stop moving and never stop learning. They saw me engaging in the community around me and getting involved. They saw me setting goals for myself and working hard to achieve them. They saw me practicing with them and learning from them just as much as they were learning from me. Most importantly, I found myself again.

I signed my children up for karate so they could find confidence and community and challenge themselves to learn skills that will help them be successful throughout their entire lives. What I hadn't realized was that "their entire lives" could just as easily start at 38 as it does at 8, and that it could apply to me as well. That's the advice I'd like to share with moms of any age or stage, and the advice I should have taken earlier myself. Or maybe I learned it at precisely the right time.

Now I'm asked when my next belt test or tournament will be and how my progression in my training is going. I have a collection of Bo staffs and Kali sticks stored in various locations throughout my house and more often than not, in the trunk of my car, which are great conversation starters. I have classes and tournament schedules on my calendar, and dear friends I text when I'm stressed about belt testing or have a question about a form. But I also text them when I want to share a joke, or confide in them when I've had a particularly rough day, or simply to share an observation about a movie I like. Maybe even something about *Cars*.

Martha Long

There are so many times you will feel you have failed, but in the eyes, heart and mind of your child, you are supermom.

Stephanie Precourt

My Journey From Smelly Kellie to Master Kellie

In 1979, I was 9 years old, and my family moved to a small agricultural town, where half the people were related, and the other half knew each other practically from birth. I was definitely the outsider and treated as such. Not only was I the "new kid" but I wore glasses, my name rhymed with "smelly", and I lived on a small dairy farm. Now living on a dairy farm was not unusual in this town but working on the farm as a girl certainly was.

My father, who always dreamed about owning a farm, had absolutely no knowledge about farming and continued to work a full-time day job, which meant my 7-year-old brother and I were the hired (unpaid) workers. Every morning before school we had to go out to the barn and do chores which included hand shoveling manure, throwing hay bales, milking, feeding, etc.   After school was a repeat of morning chores and then weekends or vacations meant more work.   My father would tell me, "If you want to work in a man's world…. you need to know how to work like a man." So, I worked right alongside him and did all the laborious tasks required for farming.

I couldn't go to my friends' houses because chores had to be done. I could have friends come over, but my father would put them to work – needless to say friends didn't come over more than once. I was a girl who was not doing girlish things and didn't act like the girls around me. Girls wouldn't allow me to hang out with them because I wasn't "girlish" enough and boys weren't kind to me when I chose to play kickball or whatever sport with them because I wasn't "boyish" enough. I was constantly bullied and picked on.

I was the kid who when I got on the school bus every kid would move over to sit by the aisle so I wouldn't have a seat until the bus driver made someone move.   I would often get into fights defending myself. It was made very clear to me each day that I wasn't welcome. This was the start of my journey into low self-esteem and self-worth.

Two years later, my dad decided I needed to learn some self-defense and through his day job knew Rick Dion, who had an ITF TaeKwonDo school in our area. This was a huge treat as we often were not allowed to do any extracurricular activities. I remember walking in and noticing that there weren't any other kids besides my brother and me, and although the class was mainly male, there were a couple of women. I was so excited to see physically strong women being accepted and part of the class. Everyone would support and celebrate their strengths and physical abilities, not make them feel weird. It was the first time in my life that I felt good at something and that it was okay to be strong and to be a fighter.

We continued to train for a couple of years. My dad even joined us in class and is now one of my favorite memories as it truly was the only nonworking thing I ever did with him. I even participated in a tournament and won my first trophy –

I had fallen in love with taekwondo and couldn't wait for the "next class." I found my peeps and I was feeling better about myself. But unfortunately, the day-to-day farm needs took priority and we had to quit.

I held on to that feeling of acceptance in the years that followed and hoped that someday I would find my flock where I would belong again. I did eventually find some friends in high school and joined the "drama" click, which was a good fit for a while. I still struggled with low self-esteem, which I think most people do in high school, but I continued to believe that I was worthless.

One day walking to class as a sophomore at the University of Vermont, I saw a flyer offering TaeKwonDo lessons and decided to go. I met the students, who immediately welcomed me, and the instructor was a student of now Master Rick Dion. Master Dion was now running two TaeKwonDo Schools with his wife (also black belt) Laurie Dion.   I was ecstatic that I would be seeing him again. Reuniting with Master Dion was an important event in my life journey as it felt like a family reunion. I hadn't realized at the time what a huge impact both he and especially Mrs. Dion would have on my life going forward.

Flash forward a couple of years, I continued training – found training as a twenty-year-old was way different than a 9-year-old. I still had bouts of depression as I was putting myself through school and again felt I wasn't good enough and became a cutter to punish myself for my "failures".   I started working for the Dions as their secretary at the dojang, I now had a front-seat view of what it was like running a martial arts school and I had the opportunity to work beside one of the highest-ranking women in the state of VT.

The Dions became my family – Master Dion was like an uncle/father figure to me whom I wanted to make proud. But it was Mrs. Dion who was my real mentor and idol…much later a big sister. I admired her for paving the way for other women in the martial arts. It was the late 80s and still martial arts were considered a male sport/activity. We would attend tournaments and most of the judges were men as were competitors – Mrs. Dion was one of the very few head refs and competitors (and she often won).

Mrs. Dion as a co-owner of a school was huge and she was an amazing mentor to so many women. Our school had about 50% women – many of them coming from other schools I believe due in part to Mrs. Dion. She represented us and showed us what we were capable of. Sometimes at tournaments men and women black belts would compete in the same division for forms/katas, and how exciting it would be when she would win. She really demonstrated that yes, women do belong in the martial arts, and yes, we could compete, own schools, be master instructors, and succeed. I wouldn't be where I am today, without her guiding light.

I decided at about 2nd degree black belt that my dream was to become a master instructor (4th degree) and own a taekwondo school. I continued working for the Dions in the evenings, started teaching kids' classes and training while working full time at the college. I survived some rather big injuries – a knee replacement (back then was a big deal – not like it is today), was told NO TaeKwonDo for a year but returned sooner due to working so hard at PT and severed hamstring injury. Unfortunately, this was just the beginning of my path with surgeries and injuries, and I was later diagnosed with fibromyalgia. It would have been so easy after each injury to say I'm done, I can't fight back anymore, but the need to do taekwondo overpowered my fear of recovering from another surgery/injury.

Around 1998, I was a 3rd degree black belt and the Dions were moving to South Carolina to fulfill their own dream and to open a school there. Honestly, part of me was crushed. Taekwondo had become a huge part of who I was, and I had never done it without the Dions. I felt lost. I ended up taking a new job that required me to move a couple of hours away from the school, still attempted to go to class a couple of times a month but the spark and drive were gone. I think because of the pain I felt with the Dions leaving I decided I'd be done with the martial arts. I had a new career, a new home at a big dairy farm with my future husband, and was getting married – it was time to move on.

I threw away all my uniforms (but my original Dion's black trim uniform which my daughter wears occasionally) and my belts. Trying to convince myself I didn't need taekwondo in my life. I think it was more so that I would no longer see these things and be reminded about what I was missing. I decided to focus on my new life and walked away from taekwondo. It was time to grow up, put my dream away, and support my husband and children, which I think is how a lot of moms feel. Our hopes and dreams come after everyone else's. My lack of self-esteem and self-worth made this decision easy because others mattered more than me.

Once my daughter, Megan, was born, I had to stop working on the farm due to her health issues and became a stay-at-home mom. I never thought I'd be happy doing something like that, but I totally was. I loved being a mom and a couple years later our family grew to 4 with the addition of my son, Ryan. I created a position with a local dairy grain company so that I could work at home to be with the kids and still be able

to take them to several activities. Every day we had a class to
attend – gymnastics, music, Spanish, art, etc. – I was a stay-at-
home mom, but we didn't stay home much. I wanted to give
my kids a chance to explore things and sports because I never
did, and they were like sponges and were able to learn so
many things – plus it was fun.

Megan was determined to be exceptionally gifted through
testing but was also, as time went on, diagnosed with OCD
(obsessive-compulsive disorder) and anxiety. This later lead
to more diagnoses of depression and ADH – as a young adult
now we finally have the right diagnosis of level one autism.
So, I learned a lot about teaching, listening, etc. through
working with Megan. She was my intellectually driven child
and of course, Ryan was the complete opposite. He was all
physical – learning to walk at 7 months …. well truthfully it
was more like learning to run. Ryan could just naturally do
anything physical. So, I also learned a lot through him, how
to keep a physically charged individual focused. Looking
back now I can see how my kids were truly my first
"students" and taught me how to instruct. I also watched
how other people taught the kids' programs, the games they
played, the expectations they had, and how they kept kids
focused and engaged.

I was pretty convinced that I was done with taekwondo….
but apparently taekwondo wasn't done with me. Megan
attended a private school and on Fridays, it was "athletic day"
where they would spend most of the day learning and playing
different sport-like/physical activities. Due to her anxiety,
Fridays were tough for her first year there as a kindergartener
and every Thursday night she would have a mini breakdown.
She didn't know what the activity was, didn't already know
how to do it, and didn't know if she would be any good at it.

One Thursday night she came home and told me they were going to be doing taekwondo, which obviously piqued my interest as I had been looking for a school to enroll her in. The next morning, I asked the teacher about it and found out it was actually Tai Chi they were supposed to be doing but the teacher had to back out. Without even thinking I blurted out that years ago I used to do this martial art called taekwondo and that I was a black belt. So, if they ever need an activity just let me know. His reply was, "What are you doing next Friday?" So open mouth, insert foot.

After about 8 years I was going to teach taekwondo again. I didn't have a uniform, no kicking paddles, and no idea what I was going to do. It was complicated more by the fact that the preschool was very nontraditional with teachers being referred to by first name, less structured, mixed school with kids from kindergarten through 6th grade and several of the older kids were experts in "eye-rolling". All that week I struggled with how to have the kids address me, how structured/strict I would be and how much would they hate it. I ultimately decided that I had to teach it the way I knew how and started off class explaining that during class they were to address me as Mrs. Danyow (I was still married at the time) and ma'am. They were going to learn about bowing, line up by rank, and would be respectful.

I truly believe I blew some of their minds that day, but we continued to have a total of 3 classes as it was at the end of the school year. I really enjoyed it. I figured I would do a couple more classes for them next year if they wanted but had no plans on doing more than that. At the time I was still home with Ryan, who was two, subbing at Megan's school, taking the kids to their extra activities, and was still working from home. The home job had become almost full time and

I had to work crazy hours – 5 AM before kids awoke, during Ryan's nap time, and evenings after they were in bed. Absolutely no time for anything else.

During our end-of-the-school-year picnic, a mom approached me and said her son absolutely loved taekwondo and would like to continue. I told her that I would search and see if I could find a school for him. She corrected me and said he wanted to train with me only. Her son was one of the best "eye-rollers" in the school and was the one I was most worried about teaching due to the attitude I often witnessed. (**Spoiler Alert – he became my first black belt).   She later explained to me that he had stopped doing all extracurricular activities, and used to love baseball because his stepbrother had committed suicide and he basically shut down and was obviously struggling with so many things.

Another mom overheard us talking and said her son wanted the same thing. He was extremely intelligent and had never gotten involved with any physical activity. She was shocked that he wanted to also do taekwondo. Needless to say, my head was spinning. What just happened!! I was done with taekwondo and totally "content" with my new life…...which of course was a lie, but we tell ourselves we are fine often for the sake of our family. Our kids come first…our spouse comes first…. our home duties come first…. our kids' school duties come first…. doctor appointments…. grocery shopping…. dishes…. laundry…..work…. wife responsibilities…. How could I be so selfish that I would ignore all these responsibilities and teach again!!! I struggled with the decision all summer and finally decided that "if you have students…. you must teach". Plus, I informed my spouse I would get paid for these classes, which helped convince him that I could do this.

The first week of school, I announced that I would be teaching two taekwondo classes in the "big room" two afternoons a week right after school – first class for K-1 and second class for 2-6 grades. I was so nervous for my first day and to my surprise, I had 3 for the first class (my daughter included – who was so excited) and 5 in the second class.

I continued to just teach at the private school as Ryan was still just in preschool, even had my first adult join (she was a mom) and it was all that I had time for, but it was great. A huge learning curve as I had to relearn all the forms, learn how to hold boards, order supplies, run testings, set up an actual business, and all the pieces that go along with that. One of the hardest things was coming up with a name. I didn't want to name it after the town I was teaching in (in case I ever changed location) and I didn't want to use my last name. My daughter had recently taught me about acrostic poems, so I put my brain to the test. Asked myself why was I teaching again? What did I really want my students to learn? That's how I came up with the name TaeKwonDo K.I.C.K.S. – Keep fit, Inner strength, Confidence, Kinship and Self-defense. At that moment I realized my real reason for teaching was that I wanted to help increase my students' confidence, inner strength, and self-worth and to feel welcomed and important. All the things I wish I had – I still to this day suffer from low self-esteem.

During this time, I also had my first hip replacement – which of course threw a monkey wrench into the system and put me once again at a crossroad. Do I just pack it up and stop? Or do I fight back and work hard so I can teach again? I decided on the latter and went back to teach two weeks post-surgery using a walker. I moved to a new bigger location and was now accepting students that were not just associated with the private school. Things were looking up for me.…...so I thought.

The next year, Ryan started Kindergarten, which meant I would be looking for a full-time job outside of the home as my husband and I had discussed. It was the first week of school, returned home from bringing the kids to school and my husband was waiting for me in the kitchen. I thought he was just home for breakfast; he owned the farm with his father, and it was a big dairy farm. At the time they were milking close to a thousand cows, and he was slowly in the process of buying it. However, his reason for being home was to tell me he was leaving me as he needed to end our marriage before moving forward with buying the farm.

Prior to this, we had a recent fight (which was unusual for us – we didn't fight, but we also weren't as close anymore, as my focus was the kids and his was the farm). I mentioned wanting to go away for a weekend – he said no and that I couldn't use any of the credit cards, although he could because I wasn't working. He vehemently asked – How much are you making with taekwondo anyway? I realize now he was just picking a fight to have an excuse to leave as I later found out he had been unfaithful all summer, but attacking my decision to teach always stuck with me.

I think I decided right then and there that someday my taekwondo business would be successful, whereas before it was more of a hobby. He also never believed I had fibromyalgia and just thought I was lazy. I told him if I "got" the kids I would walk away from the farm. Without hesitation he agreed, so I was then granted sole custody of Megan and Ryan, but I was also going to have to be without them on Saturday as that was his visitation day. The idea of not having my kids around nearly crushed me. We were always together and especially to be without them on Saturday when we would often plan fun events and just be able to crash and hang out as a family.

Instead of sitting around the house depressed on Saturday mornings, I decided to open a 2nd KICKS location teaching on Saturdays and Tuesdays. This would still give me Wednesday and Thursday nights at home with my kids. It turned out to be a great decision not only because I wasn't sitting home depressed, but it became my largest school and still is today. So, I was able to take a potentially emotionally crushing experience into a win due to taekwondo.

A month after the separation, my instructor – Mrs. Dion – flew in to test me for 4th Degree (Master Instructor). I was honored that she would make the trip just for me and I was going to achieve the final goal of becoming a master. During the testing though I landed wrong after a jump and blew out my right knee and left in an ambulance. So again, I was facing the decision – Do I just stop doing taekwondo? Do I really have the strength to recover again from a major surgery? Is it even a wise decision since I now had the sole responsibility of raising my children? I ultimately decided to keep teaching and went through rehab again. The orthopedic surgeon wanted to operate but I said I couldn't due to having full custody and couldn't afford to take time off to recover. I also then needed to find full-time work as well.

I did find a full-time job (with the company I had been working from home with) that was understanding about my taekwondo business and being a single parent. They allowed me to rearrange my office hours to make my other commitments and I made up the time by working at home. This continued for a few years and during that time I had the other hip replaced and eventually had to have emergency

surgery on the knee I injured back at testing. This was such a
difficult time. I was trying to not only balance two jobs,
while trying to also grow KICKS by doing after-school
programs and increasing the number of classes offered per
night, but also making sure I was fulfilling my job as the only
parent and being able to financially support us. I now had a
mortgage, utilities, private school tuition, and all the other
daily expenses.

Eventually, I was at a crossroads between giving up TKD so I
could take a promotion at my day job…. or quit my day job
and focus on TKD entirely because it had grown to a point
where I could no longer do both. So, I took the giant leap of
faith against everyone else's opinion, including my folks, and
decided to focus on KICKS. My kids were absolutely great
during all this, understanding I couldn't attend all their
practices or games, having to come to hang out while I
taught, and knowing at night, I still had work to do. Megan
continued to train with me, and I saw how much she gained
from TKD. Also, my kids were proud of me for following
my dream. They were able to see that with hard work and
determination, you can make dreams come true, which I
believe was an important lesson for them to learn.

Soon I would receive the funniest piece of mail ever…my
first metal hip was recalled! Yup just like a car part. I didn't
have it re-replaced immediately because it wasn't causing
issues but eventually, it would and unfortunately would cause
permanent damage – I can no longer bend my knee or lift my
leg to a 90 degree, which certainly makes doing TKD difficult
and painful. So again, what do I do? Keep doing TKD
although most nights I need to physically pull myself into the
house? Or decide this is the end of the road for me? I did

succeed in making my business successful – when do I say enough is enough?

Needless to say, I am still kicking and most importantly teaching others how to kick. At present time KICKS has the most students ever (about 250), I am teaching at four preschools weekly, doing sporadic after-school programs, and have four locations. My kids are now young adults, so we made it as a family too. I have also remarried, to someone who allows me to be who I am, also does TKD, and is supportive. My left knee has been replaced, with the right knee heading that way soon along with my right shoulder. Eventually, my hips will need to be redone – as they only last about 15 years. Students tease me and say I'm going to become RoboMom.

I am unfortunately starting to plan for retirement as my body just can't take it much longer, but I will be forever grateful for all that the martial arts have given me. It gave me a family when I needed it most whether healing from a divorce or surgery. I joke and often tell all my students that they are also "my children" regardless of their age.   It gave me direction when I felt like I was just floundering. It gave me strength when I was feeling my weakest. It has allowed me to pay it forward by hopefully helping others to find their inner strength and confidence.

Being a martial artist helped me be a better mom. I believe working with students with various learning styles and physical abilities helped me be able to understand my kids and communicate with them better. Megan trained with me, which was an amazing and difficult experience at times, but I believe it is part of the reason we have a strong relationship. She trained until middle school, receiving her 2nd degree, and although she isn't currently training anymore it is still a big part of who she is. She is very proud of being a black belt and proud of what I have accomplished.

I will admit being a woman school owner was tough as I often felt like I was on the outside looking in. Multiple times male school owners would offer to help me and when I would turn them down would feel offended and ultimately thought I was being arrogant. However, honestly, I was doing very well on my own, doing my own thing, and was satisfied with where I was. It was also funny that they never really learned what I was doing, nor did they ever think to ask me for help, thinking I didn't have anything to offer. I eventually realized I needed to leave that organization to be my true self and create the type of school I wanted.   I have been flying free since, with no instructor anymore (as the Dions have retired and Master Dion passed away a few years ago), and couldn't be happier. I have recently met a group of like-minded martial artists who are truly welcoming and supportive, which is empowering.

I hope my story helps other martial arts moms out there. I think Winnie the Pooh says it best in this quote: "You're braver than you believe, and stronger than you seem and smarter than you think". Reach for the stars and remember to be a guiding light to others.

Kellie Thomas

Successful mothers are not the ones that never struggled. They are the ones that never give up, despite the struggles.

Sharon Jaynes

Feeding My Soul

As someone born in the early 80's, I was raised in the era of
Bruce Lee films, the Karate Kid saga, Teenage Mutant Ninja
Turtles, and the Power Rangers. The characters in these
stories captivated me and inspired me. I was the youngest and
smallest member of my entire family, and I dreamed of
having the strength and courage that my heroes possessed.
Unfortunately, my parents wouldn't let my brother and me
take karate lessons until I was 12 years old. It's the only
athletic activity that I ever wanted to do, but my parents
feared it would only make my older brother more violent
since he already had so many behavior issues. Fortunately, it
is now understood that martial arts training does the
opposite. Regardless, I finally got to start taking lessons in
1995.

My original style was Okinawan Shorin Ryu karate. My
instructor was my hero. He was so cool and calm but could
move with such precision and power when he wanted to. I
aspired to be like him, so I practiced as often as I could. I
don't remember how long my brother trained with me, but I
believe he quit within the first year. I couldn't get enough
though and my parents were very supportive. They even set
up a training space for me in our unfinished basement. I had
mirrors on the wall, a thin layer of padded carpet on the

concrete floor, and my own freestanding punching bag. It was my sanctuary.

Martial arts was always a very individual activity for me. I didn't have many classmates, especially none that were my age. I didn't know at the time, but my instructor had just opened his school a year prior to my joining, so the student body was still very small. I never really cared who else was training with me though. I just loved learning new things and improving my skills. It wasn't until I got a little older that I wished I had my own peers training alongside me.

When I was a senior in high school, my life was beginning to fill up with more than just martial arts. I got my first real job at a sandwich shop, I became really active in my high school theatre department (on stage and backstage), and I got into my first relationship. My involvement in theatre was a great surprise even to myself, as I had been painfully shy and quiet. I credit my experiences in martial arts for that. I gained so much confidence and courage by doing things like belt tests and tournaments. But the truth was, I had to decide what to prioritize my time on. I had no peers to share my passion for martial arts with. The only other female students were a very obnoxious 12-year-old girl and a woman in her 40s who had previously trained in Taekwondo and wanted to learn something new. I chose to spend time with my friends during our last year before college. I swore to myself that I would return and earn my black belt. So, after 5 years of training, I left as a brown belt for what I thought would be a temporary break.

16 years later...I found myself in a conversation with one of my coworkers at the zoo. As I found myself telling him about how I used to do karate, I felt an overwhelming wave of sadness fall on me. It was like heartache and homesickness all

in one. I missed it so much and I felt shame and guilt that I had let my 17-year-old self down. I let my instructor down. It was like I had lost part of myself, but I began to realize that I could find myself again.

I had just finished breastfeeding my second child around the time he turned two years old. So, for five long years, I was either pregnant or breastfeeding. My body did not feel like it belonged to me, rather it was just a tool to create and feed my children and it was my job to maintain and care for it. Finally, I started to realize that it was my body again and that there were parts of me that I had forgotten about. I decided at age 33, it was time to train again.

I thought it was something I would pursue alone again, but my husband at that time decided to resume training as well. He had studied Taekwondo and Judo for a brief time in college. We found a school near our home that taught Karate, Taekwondo and Judo! It was challenging at first because we could not always find a babysitter for our 4-year-old daughter and 2-year-old son. We ended up bringing the kids with us most nights and setting them in a corner with coloring books and crayons. It didn't take long though before my daughter began mimicking the techniques she observed us doing. We signed her up for the Little Dragons class and when my son turned 3, he began taking the Tiny Tigers class.

Now the largest challenge I faced was the financial aspect of training. I was working as a zookeeper, which most people don't realize is an incredibly low-paying job even though it requires a bachelor's degree. My ex was only working part-time so he could stay home with the kids. We really couldn't afford tuition for all four of us. I cut every extra cost that I could think of. We sacrificed everything that wasn't a necessity. No fast food or eating out. No going to the movies.

No buying brand-name grocery items. We could still only afford tuition for 3 of us, so I had an honest talk with the school owner and head instructor and they let all of us train for the price of 3.

My kids loved martial arts in the beginning, but we went from being at the dojo 2 nights a week to 4 or 5 nights a week. My ex-husband and I both took on the responsibilities of teaching classes and helping run after-school and camp programs. It was challenging to find time for preparing meals and we often had to bring food for the kids with us to the dojo. My kids and my ex were feeling burned out and started to spend less time at the dojo. There were a lot of factors that led to our decision to take a break from training again, but I won't go into details. We left the school after 3 and a half years. And then a month later, the pandemic of 2020 shut everything down.

Before the pandemic, I was working as a substitute teacher in addition to working at the dojo and training 5 nights a week. I had recently left my career as a zookeeper in order to pursue a new career teaching middle school science. Teachers actually make quite a bit more money than zookeepers. I was also working out 3 days a week at a kickboxing fitness gym. Once the schools and gyms closed for Covid, my world was drastically different. I went on walks every day with my family and I tried to keep up with my kickboxing workouts online, but it wasn't the same. By the end of 2020, my life changed in almost every way. After years of trying to make my struggling marriage work, my ex and I separated. I began working as a trainer at the kickboxing gym. Becoming a teacher was no longer my goal as the schools were closed and my teacher friends grew more unsatisfied every year with the education system.

Even though I wasn't training in traditional martial arts, I was able to still feel connected to it through the kickboxing gym. All of the bag work and pad work was highly enjoyable, and I got in the best physical shape of my life, even though I was in my late thirties. It also provided me with the opportunity to continue teaching since most of the gym members had no previous experience in boxing or any other martial art. It was a change going from teaching children to only working with adults. I found that I really enjoy both, just in different ways. Kids are usually more fun, but I enjoy the depth of learning that adults are more capable of.

During that time, I also began taking lightsaber stage combat classes at a local HEMA school. My friend and I thought it would be fun and we were proven correct. It was way outside my comfort zone but still reminded me of my traditional martial arts training combined with my time in theatre. We got to perform at some local events, and I challenged myself to learn as many fun tricks as possible. That was when I started to make fun videos online, that I honestly didn't expect anyone to watch. I was wrong thankfully, because one of those people who found my videos is now my current husband.

We were part of a small group of strangers on TikTok who made our own community. Some of us were martial artists, some were just there to have fun with lightsabers, and some were both. The man who is now my husband invited me to travel across the country to attend the 35th-anniversary celebration at his home dojo. I hadn't been to a traditional karate school in almost two years, so I was excited for the opportunity.

I honestly fell in love with Victor before I ever met him in person, but that trip confirmed everything. We spent one year in a long-distance relationship. I made four trips out to New Jersey to see him over that time. We always spent at least 2 of my nights at the dojo. When he moved to Kansas to be with me, we didn't know what the future would hold for our martial arts journey.

Victor began teaching me his style of karate, while he cross-trained online with his kung fu instructor. We decided that we wanted to start teaching together six months after his arrival. We rented a room in a church one night a week. Our first students were mostly friends of my son, who was 8, and some children of an old friend who saw my social media posts. We loved getting to teach together but felt too limited by not having our own space.

Six months later, we got married and opened our own commercial dojo. We went from one night a week to 6 days of teaching. I still work a full-time job at a pet store, so Victor handles most of the business aspects of our dojo. We teach together though. Our dream is to make martial arts a full-time job for both of us. My children, however, don't share the same dream.

When we were only teaching once a week, my kids participated and seemed to really enjoy training again. Now we are teaching 4 nights a week and they are with us every other week. We told them that we'll never force them to train, so we made a special place for them in the back room of the dojo where a water heater used to be. They each have a desk and comfortable chair so they can do schoolwork or just play on their electronics. We are 6 months in, and my daughter has decided to stop training for now. My son will only take classes on the nights his friends are there. It makes me a little sad, but I am hopeful that they will both become more involved in the future.

In the meantime, I will continue to improve myself through my martial arts. I am setting an example for my kids. By following my passion, even though it is not always convenient, my kids can see what it means to sacrifice and prioritize in order to achieve one's goals. I hope my children find things that they are passionate about, even if it isn't martial arts.

And that was my long story short.

Now here is my advice…

To the mothers:

Do not neglect the parts of yourself that feed your soul and fuel your passions. You were not always a mother. Take time for yourself even if it makes you feel a little guilty. You are still worth investing in and you have more personal growth ahead of you. Think about the kind of person you hope for your child to grow up to be. Be that kind of person. They are watching you. They are learning from you. What kind of example are you presenting to them? Do you hope they will become the best version of themselves? You need to be the best version of yourself too.

To everyone else:

Do not look at the mothers in your life and forget that they are more than just that. They are whole and complete human beings just like you. They carry the great responsibility of raising children (just like dads) but they can carry it better if they take time to care for themselves too. I'm not talking about a spa day. I'm talking about self-improvement. It might be martial arts, or writing, or music, or whatever helps them be their best. Remind them to take time to work on that, and praise them for it.

Karen Guarino

Black Belt Grandmom

Barbara Wood moved from London to Bristol, UK, to be near her grandsons, Dylan and Ash, when they were young.

She then took them along to Taekwondo classes and thought 'this looks good'. When she asked if there was an age limit and they said no, she decided to join in.

She took up the Korean martial art at the age of 68 and seven years later achieved her black belt, aged 75.

She said: "I figured if I didn't give it a go, I'd just be at home vegetating – rather than in the dojang meditating.

"I think age is just a number and you shouldn't think you're not capable of doing something just because you're old.

"I think it's important to give things a go and if it doesn't suit you, you can give it up – but you must try."

She has a special bond with her grandsons, which she believes has been cemented through their martial arts training together.

She said: "We have a great bond and we'll always have it, even as they grow up and become more independent.

"I think as a grandparent you have more time and less responsibility, so your time together is less strict and more relaxed than it would be if you were the parent."

Dylan no longer does martial arts but catches up with his grandmother on a weekly basis.

Ash, who started at the age of seven and is now 15, has jokingly referred to his grandmother 'Mr. Miyagi' during training.

Barbara said: "Dylan and I have different interests, which is nice. Ash and I train together weekly, but though we're in the same class, we tend to practice independently.

"He has his friends and I think it's important that he goes on his own journey, so I don't interfere. We still have fun together and challenge each other.

"He has called me 'Mr. Miyagi,' but in reality, he doesn't want me to teach him. Besides, I'd rather lead by example than instruction.

"I think martial arts instil respect and discipline, which is good for children to learn from a young age – both in the training hall and outside.

"It also emphasizes the importance of perseverance, which is necessary in all areas of life. I don't give up easily and neither do they.

"I'm proud of them and they both think it's marvelous that I've gained my black belt. I think it's shown them what's possible when you put your mind to it."

Only around two percent of students who take up martial arts attain a black belt, which takes years to achieve.

The International Taekwondo Federation (ITF) says black belts are expected to have developed proficiency and a thorough understanding of all color belt gradings, as well as their own.

Students have to carry out advanced patterns, sparring, self-defense, and breaking, as well as understand the theory behind the Korean martial art.

Barbara, who is also a green belt in Tang Soo Do, another Korean-based martial art, said: "I am proud of my black belt after working so hard for all those years.

"Once I got over my nerves, everything fell into place. I was the only one to break everything, I did well in sparring, and my line work was fine.

"I also got 80 percent right in my theory questions. I spent weeks going through it so it was all in my head."

She started at Fishponds Taekwondo Academy and then joined Thornbury Taekwondo for extra tuition.

She came under the instruction of Master Vaughan Buxton, a 7th-degree black belt and a British, European, and World title holder, who believed in her ability to achieve a black belt.

She said: "He told me it was my journey and was very encouraging. We all have different abilities, but with commitment and hard work, it's possible to improve and reach your goals. But sometimes it's a marathon and not a sprint."

Barbara was born in 1948 in post-war Britain in Wandsworth, South London, and was brought up with traditional views on a woman's role in the family at that time.

She was married and had her first child while a teenager. She divorced in 1972, then met someone else, and had two more children. She stopped working for a time while raising them.

Barbara, who managed bookkeeping at a jewelry store, said: "We were told as children that women get married and have children. I wasn't encouraged to continue my studies or develop a career."

The Suffragettes taught themselves the martial art of Jiu-Jitsu in the early 1900s. And a feminist self-
defense movement emerged in the 1970s because of violence against women.

Women appeared in combative arts in film in the 1940s, while so many men went off to war. In the 1980s Hong Kong action films featured heroines such as Cynthia Rothrock and Michelle Yeoh.

Barbara said: "When I was growing up, we didn't see women in martial arts. There are lots of women in martial arts now and our classes reflect this. I think it's good for girls and women to learn a martial art as it gives them self-defense skills and confidence."

Barbara, a talented gymnast and speed skater in her youth, credits the martial art with boosting her fitness and memory.

She said: "It not only helps to keep you physically fit, but mentally sharp too."

Research suggests martial arts improve mobility, flexibility, balance, and coordination in older adults. It also engages the mind and has been found to have therapeutic benefits.

Barbara also enjoys the social side at the club, where she is affectionately known as 'the old lady.'

She said: "We take the class seriously but also have a laugh and some banter. As there are students in their 50s and 60s, I don't feel out of place.

"I'd recommend it to anyone. There's no age limit and you just do what you can. I find it fun and very rewarding."

Mr Buxton said: "Barbara has impressed everyone at the club with her dedication and hard work. She's an inspiration and shows that taekwondo is suitable for people of all ages."

Barbara Wood, interview by Angela Belassie

To describe my mother would be to write about a hurricane in its perfect power. Or the climbing, falling colors of a rainbow.

Maya Angelou

Balancing Act

"Are you and Gunnar related?" I'm hurrying through the stands at a tournament, trying to see as many of my students as I can while I wait for my own event to start when the question comes. I turn and find one of the parents of a member of the junior demo team approaching me. I answer in the affirmative, but don't offer any details.

"Is he your son?" she presses, standing beside me. I pause for a split second, then tell her that yes, he is my son, and again don't volunteer any other information. It's not that I'm not proud of my son - his work with our junior demo team as their head coach has me absolutely bursting with pride. It's the fact that we were still trying to figure out our relationship at the studio with him a moody and independent teenager, and myself as the studio's program director and one of the instructors. It was a very delicate balancing act with rules that seemed to change daily. Just when I thought I'd got my feet under me, they're getting swept again.

And just like any martial artist improving their skills, I kept learning counters and new stances as the old ones got challenged. And my son kept learning new ways to challenge me as he tried to find himself. It was exhausting, but worth it at the same time, especially once we finally found the balance we needed together.

While I was the one who began martial arts first in our family (well, actually it was my brother, but going back 30 years to the beginning of my journey, I don't think anyone is going to quibble with a few months of time) my son was the first one to join our studio. My genetic medical condition had stopped my formal training as a teenager, and while I kept my hand in kickboxing and taking the odd class when I could, I had stopped testing at 3rd kyu. So when my young son had wanted to try karate, I was open to the idea, and eventually found the place that would become a second home to us all - Karate International of Windham under Shihan Joe Costa.

Gunnar was a natural, taking to the sport quickly and meeting every evaluation on time and with flying colors. He joined the junior demo team, then the senior demo team, and finally received his junior Black Belt in just four years. He loved the sport, and I loved cheering him on. I was also secretly jealous - I missed it. I had done some kickboxing over the years, but never went back to formal lessons because I was sure it would be impossible with my condition. In fact, shortly after he began his training, an accident during kickboxing led to my condition progressing rapidly, and my needing a wheelchair for a while as I fought to regain strength.

But shortly before Gunnar achieved 3rd kyu, the pandemic hit and the way that he trained changed. Suddenly, classes were in our living room over Zoom, and to do partner work, he had to bring someone with him to outdoor classes once weekly. Well, I was the one with the background, so I was the one who went with him to these classes. Nervous as hell, and worried about what would happen if my body couldn't handle the strain. I was walking on my own again at this point, but had one leg in a metal brace.

Apparently, I didn't need to worry. My body handled things fine, and what was more, deep muscle memory started to come to the surface. My son was working on his latest form - the last form in fact that I had learned before stopping all those years ago. I was doing it with him when Shihan Joe approached, a strange look on his face.

"Have you done karate before?" he asked me with a smile. I replied that I had, and he said that he could tell - I had the stances, strikes, and hand positions all correct - which I now realize would have been a little weird to see a total beginner exhibiting in a fairly advanced form! And none of this was conscious. I didn't even know I was chambering my hands until it was pointed out to me. It did start to spark something new, though.

Those early morning classes together made me realize how much I had truly missed my own practice. I talked with Gunnar, and my husband Pär, and decided to sign up for a month of lessons. Pär joined me, and Gunnar worked with me to practice in the afternoons after we were done with homeschool.

Shihan Joe had generously offered me my old rank back, but I wanted to earn it. I asked him to give me a month of study, and then to evaluate me; I would accept whatever rank he felt I deserved, even if it was 10th kyu.

At the end of the month, I was pleasantly surprised to find that I had enough knowledge to officially restart at 5th kyu rank - our school's Green belt. I was also given the opportunity to advance more quickly until I regained 3rd -

about 6 more months - before I slowed down to the pace that was more normal at our school.

At first, things were great. Pär, Gunnar, and myself all attended our regular classes and tests. We trained together at home, took our separate classes, and talked about the sport when the topic came up. Then, the cracks began.

First, I asked about weapons training, something I had only just begun all those years ago. It wasn't something offered to adults at the time, and I was interested. Gunnar was very good, and very advanced, taking some of the most advanced weapons classes the school offered. Shihan graciously offered to allow me to join Gunnar in those classes, as he didn't have a weapons program for adults. The reason for my joining that particular class was because it had 3 students in it. The pandemic was still raging, and class sizes were restricted. It made sense for me to attend this one, which was small, especially since I could share a smaller space with Gunnar if need be. Trying to fit me into a beginner class - all of which were much more full - would be harder.

This rankled with my then 11-year-old. He had earned the right to be in that class - I hadn't. Yet. I have since earned my right to attend those classes - and still do - but at the time, he was correct. I hadn't put the time in that he had. But I wanted to get the training, so we struck a compromise, and I stayed on the other end of the dojo mats and tried to be quiet and humble with my training, letting my son have the spotlight. I took his feedback on things from the weapons themselves, to how I interacted with the other students and instructors.

Things settled slightly, but it turned into the first of many small things we would have to begin navigating together.

6 months later, I tested for 2nd kyu and my son received his junior Black Belt. I felt that we were finally on firmer ground with one another, but apparently not. I was starting to get some recognition for my hard work at the school, and this rankled my 12-year-old even more. Karate had been his thing, and while he was fine with my taking classes, he was less fine with my excelling. He seemed to find it to be a competition between us - something that had never crossed my mind. I was simply enjoying myself, and finding joy in the completion of a very long-held goal. There is no cache in getting to your Brown belt and then stopping. In fact, there's a little shame in it. I worked very hard for years, then quit at the finish line, it is how it felt. But I had never imagined I'd be able to finish.

Every day that I get to train is a gift with my condition. I was never sure how long I would be able to continue - I'm still not, but I take it one day at a time - and I worked my hardest to get the most out of it, so if the day came when I had to hang up my gi, I would have no regrets to look back on. I really wanted that Black Belt, starting again after so long had lit a fire inside me that was all-consuming. I wanted to get that belt or die in the process, something that my son seemed to understand - he could tell how much I loved it. He just didn't love that we were now occupying the same training space.

Oddly, Gunnar didn't have the same issues with his dad, who was progressing slowly through his own journey up the ranks. Instead, Gunnar and I tease him all the time - we thought he'd stop at 6th kyu, and he has made it to 3rd with a goal of continuing. He takes our ribbing in stride, telling us that he could still quit any day.

I tried my best to give Gunnar space during this time, taking separate classes anytime I got a chance, and asking his input on things before I undertook them as a way of showing him respect - after all, he had led the way. I was trying to give him the respect I felt he deserved and nothing more. The balancing act had gotten underway - I couldn't let him take more than he deserved or push me around, showing me disrespect while I tried to calm his anxiety. But I also couldn't ignore his very real feelings either.

Then things really began to change, and the pitching surface we were navigating began to heave in earnest. I received my Black Belt, followed a few weeks later with an award for being Student of the Year.

I began assisting in classes and taking over the running of the junior/adult classes. My passion for the sport made me happy, and I wanted to give back to the community that I found so much joy in. My son meanwhile had a medical setback and had to leave all sports for several months. Things at home were also bleak; I was laid off from my job and Gunnar was in agonizing pain all the time. Trying to do the things he loved, like performing on the demo team would leave him flat on the couch for days afterward. My husband was also working many hours at a job he hated, coming home exhausted and making it to classes about one day a week on average. Our entire household felt tense, and the only thing I really felt good about was my training.

By the time surgery was over, and Gunnar was healthy and ready to return, I was working at the studio as the program director as well as an instructor. This was a huge career change for me, but I have never been happier with my work. I trained hard as well, taking many classes a week and attending as many outside events as I could get to. I've never in my life known how to not throw anything but my whole self into something, and this was no different. I was terrified that I would not be able to keep up physically with the demands, but loved my new job so much that I was doing everything I could to make it work. Life looked very different than it had just one year ago, and it was thrilling and scary at the same time.

And on top of it, and dimming my happiness a little, was the fact that Gunnar was still struggling. My now teenager was trying to come back to the place where he had once been on top, only to find his mother there. He was happy for me that I was happy and accomplishing my goals, but it was weird for him, too. Those 10 months he was gone made him feel like a stranger coming back to the place where he had once been his happiest.

It didn't help that while he'd been out, other major changes had occurred in our studio as well. The curriculum that he - and I - had studied on our journey to Black Belt had been changed. Gunnar has argued that the new curriculum isn't as good as the old and thinks it will hurt students' progress. (He has been told that he will be invited to the meeting when we assess the curriculum at the end of its first complete cycle if he still cares enough to do so). This curriculum change doesn't impact him as a Black Belt, but it does include things he didn't need to learn previously, which leaves him an odd place now. Does he learn it? Pick up where he left off?

The junior demo team was gone, the pandemic having killed it, and the senior team seemed - to Gunnar - to be suffering for it. Many people he had known and loved had also left during the pandemic and had been replaced with people he didn't know. He wanted to quit completely, but I stopped him. Right before he had gone on leave, it was time for his contract renewal. I had asked him if he wanted to renew - it was a three-year commitment - and he said yes. In fact, his exact words were that he wanted to commit and receive his next rank. Since the contract would extend to shortly after he turned 16, he could get his next rank as a full Black Belt, rather than junior, something that had some appeal for him. This was shortly followed by his decision to have surgery - his goal and reason for having the surgery was to return and rejoin the senior demo team.

I reminded him of these commitments and told him that I'd support him in any way I could, but that he had to return. It was a life lesson, I told him - you follow through on your commitments. I also told him to find something that he could do within the studio or his training that would make him feel better about it, and that I'd do my best to keep us separate.

This was followed by many bumps, some small, some big. Working and training at the studio, I'm there a lot. And Gunnar didn't want to be taught by his mother - during his time off, I'd surpassed him in knowledge. This rankled. He also didn't want people to know about our relationship if they didn't already. He wanted space, and I wanted him to have it if it would help keep the peace. I did my best, always referring to him as Mr. Gunnar or Senior Sempai Gunnar if he was assisting in a class, and if I had to teach part of a class he was in, I tried to find another instructor to work with him whenever possible.

It wasn't all constant bumps and bruises, though. There have been some great times, too, such as at the last Mother's Day class, when he passionately insisted I learn a staff trick (Bo is not my weapon, but it is Gunnar's) and we cheered and he hugged me when I got it right. Gunnar makes me proud every day, but there have been few times I've been prouder than when he began advocating for the return of our junior demo team - SWAT. Gunnar was the very last member of our senior demo team STORM to be on SWAT first. He joined STORM during the pandemic, right after SWAT was ended. And he argued that STORM was better when members had to put their time in on SWAT first. He argued so long and so passionately, that he was given the opportunity to recreate SWAT, as long as he took responsibility for it, and could find an adult to assist. Because while he is a talented 14-year-old martial artist, he is still 14.

I was adamant that I would not be the one to assist. We needed space. Things were better all the time, and I was not going to be the one to rock that boat again. But one thing led to another, led to the Sensei who was going to assist suddenly being unavailable, which led to me becoming my son's assistant coach.

We talked and decided that if no one knew I was his mother, we wouldn't tell them. I would refer to him as Mr. Gunnar only and would let him take the lead. I would provide backup, along with one of our teenage assistant instructors, another STORM member who volunteered his time to help.

Anytime Gunnar couldn't attend a practice, I would step in, and read a prepared announcement from Mr. Gunnar to the team. I would preface things with, "Mr. Gunnar would like," and "Mr. Gunnar wants," trying to provide distance. Something that is not always easy, since I see these kids in class each week, and have my own relationship with them. I like to tease them, grabbing them by the shoulders when they goof off in class, and admonishing them saying that I expect better of a SWAT member. Stepping back and trying not to be that person during practice feels weird, but being myself feels like stepping on my son's toes. It doesn't help that Gunnar has a fierce independent streak (I wonder where he gets that from) and wants to do everything for himself.

Asking me - or anyone - for help doesn't come easily to him. I've bitten my tongue an awful lot during SWAT practices, but the end result has been worth it - watching my son learn to step up and lead while watching a group of hungry and talented kids learn to come together as a team.

If I have a fault (actually, I have many, but if I had to pick one to work on the most) it's that I tend to hold back. I let my nerves, anxiety, and medical condition hold me back sometimes. A coworker at the studio - rightly - called me out on that last year. Telling me that I had to stop, that I was more capable than I was showing. Ouch. But he was correct, and I decided to take that to heart.

I have told Shihan Joe to call me out if he thought that I was holding back in any way - my training, my work - and he has done so several times. I do my best to hold myself accountable and to encourage others to do so, too. As I result, I believe that I've become a better martial artist, and in many ways a better mom as well.

That is why when Gunnar told me recently that he was really only continuing his own training to make me happy, I told him it was OK to stop if he really wanted. I told him he had to finish his commitment to SWAT, as he owed it to those kids to finish what he started. But that he could step back from his own training if he wanted to. Karate makes me happy. It brings me focus and joy, and a deep, deep need to push myself as hard as I can to fight against my medical condition for just one more day on the mat. But if it doesn't make my son happy, then he needs to do what's right for him. This weird place our relationship sits in when we are at the dojo needs to be about more than that. We can't be Mama and Gunnar at home and Miss Sarabeth and Mr.

Gunnar on the mat. We have to be ourselves apart and together at all times.

Gunnar has decided to keep training, but also reserves the right to stop when he thinks the time is right. I've agreed to let him without pushback. For the first time in 4 years, the weird balance board we've stood on whenever the topic of karate has come up is still. He comes up to me smiling when he sees me, I tease him like I would at home. We both mock my husband for his strange approach to his practice of seemingly hating it while also committing more deeply with each passing month. (He'll be testing for 2nd kyu soon, and I'm finally ordering him a belt display since I think it will finally be filled. Gunnar thinks this will make him quit just to spite the display itself).

As a martial artist, instructor, and program director, I see a lot of karate moms. I've watched my best friend train with two of her daughters and seen her frustration when they try and correct her. I've seen mothers and daughters and mothers and sons on the mat together, moms holding their children accountable, and the children gleefully using their moms as targets. I've seen one mom take her teenage son to the mat with a fierce determination that frankly scares me a little. I know that we all come to the mat for different reasons. But I also know that often, we all take away with us some of the same benefits. As a very proud Karate Mom, I'm also thankful every day for the lessons I've learned on the mat that will hopefully continue to strengthen my relationship with my son as he continues to grow into a person that I am so incredibly proud to know.

Sarabeth South

*There are places in the heart you don't
even know exist until you love a child.*

Anne Lamott

Mom, Can I Take Karate?

You would not be able to tell by looking at me, but I have spent the last 18 years in martial arts, and I'm a better mom because of it. I grew up through the 1970's and 80's. I wanted to wax on/wax off with the Karate Kid and break boards with my bare hands, and karate seemed powerful and exotic. When I asked my mom if I could take karate lessons, my mom, a sensible woman of the 1950s, said flatly, "No, girls don't do karate, they do ballet." And so, ballet lessons it was, and let me tell you, I was not very good at ballet. I was the kid at the recital in the back row, all the way to the left so that only my parents would look at me. Ballet made me feel awkward and embarrassed by my body and my ability to move with any sort of grace or coordination. I quickly gave up on dance or anything that involved moving where other people could see me: aerobics, clubbing, dancing at weddings, I avoided it all.

Many years later I had a daughter of my own, and we had a beautiful karate school, or dojo, by a pond in town. My daughter and I would go down to the pond to feed the ducks and we'd watch the karate classes on Saturdays or the kendo classes on Friday nights and I'd admire their movement, thinking I could never do what they were doing. One day when my daughter was five, she said the magic words, "Mom, can we take karate lessons?" My heart skipped a beat, I wanted my daughter to know she could do whatever she set her mind to, but I would need to be brave, take a class with her regardless of feeling awkward, and share the moment with her. I chose that dojo on the pond specifically because it was a traditional style dojo - no competitions or trophies, just learning the art for the sake of personal development, good health, and character. I have nothing against good competition, but I was so uncomfortable with public movement, the idea of competition was far too intimidating for me, and this seemed like a safe way to dip a toe into the world of karate.

The dojo welcomed us in, and before we signed up, they offered us a trial class. I was so nervous to walk in, I worried about feeling awkward and making a fool of myself. But it was important to me as a mom that I show my daughter that it's OK to struggle and try something outside your comfort zone. When we arrived, a wonderful and patient teacher took us off to the side of the class and introduced us to the basic concepts of Shotokan karate stances, blocks, and strikes. Even though I wasn't a natural, that first class was magic for me. Something aligned in my soul that day, and it just felt right. Luckily my daughter also enjoyed the class, and we signed up that night.

The style of karate I study is Shotokan, a popular style of karate that has its roots in Okinawa, Japan. In fact, part of Shotokan's popularity in Japan stemmed from it being adapted to be taught to school children, with an organized curriculum that builds upon itself, and a set of precepts that builds good character, including, *'There is no first strike in Shotokan'*. As a mom and a student, I felt that it is an important lesson, there is no excuse for starting violence, but

you do have a right and ability to defend yourself. This was
not anything like what my mother's (and many other people I
have spoken with) concept of what karate was all about.

I struggled a lot in the beginning, trying to figure out which
foot and which hand goes where, but I stuck to it, and my
daughter was there with me figuring out her path as well. I
learned to be patient with myself and value my body and
what it could do with practice, and she learned focus and
strength. As I rose up the ranks, I built up my confidence, a
belief in myself I never thought possible. I stopped worrying
about being 'weird' and different from the other moms at the
PTO meetings at school. As my daughter once pointed out, I
was the only mom in the carpool line who got Japanese
weapons for Mother's Day, and she thought that was the
greatest thing ever. She saw me being my own person, and
she felt confident being her own person.

There is a Japanese phrase, 'Nana korobi, ya oki', which
translates to 'Fall down seven times, stand up eight', which is
about perseverance, about never giving up, trying again, even
when it is hard. I struggled with a lot in karate, especially
sparring, but I kept trying, I listened to my instructors, and in
time it would come. It was valuable for my daughter to see
me struggle because she saw me get back up again and again
and it made a difference in how she approached things.
There was a belt test where she had been goofing off and was
not performing to the standards for the next level. When it
came time to award the new ranks, the teacher pulled me
aside to let me know she wouldn't be promoted, giving us an
opportunity to duck out if needed. I talked to my daughter,
and she said that she wanted to stay. We did, and after the
belts were awarded, she congratulated those who passed and
kept her composure. After class I praised her bravery and

good sportsmanship, and told her how proud I was. We went home, had a good cry, and the next week she was back in class with better focus and effort, and she passed the next test with flying colors.

As time went on and my daughter moved into middle school with more homework and other activities, she eventually left karate, but the strength and character lessons she learned at the dojo stayed with her. She was never aggressive, but she could stand up for herself and would defend her friends as well. She is now a woman who knows who she is and has the courage to go after what she wants in life.

As for me, I stayed with karate and continued my journey. When I moved into brown belt, or a senior student role, I started to assist in class and learn how to give back through teaching. In my dojo, part of earning your black belt is to spar with every person in the dojo who comes to your test. When the time for my test came, my daughter returned to the dojo and suited up. In the midst of the most nerve-wracking experience, there was my girl, the one who had invited me to try karate with her so many years before, both sparring and supporting me. As a mom, I could not have been more proud to have her there with me.

Turning the corner to black belt was not the end of my journey, but rather the beginning of a new one – teaching. It was now my role to get students, especially kids, excited and engaged with the concepts we were teaching. I would take those who were struggling off to the side and give them one-to-one support and encouragement. I would also keep them in line when they got rowdy with "Don't make me use my Mom Voice!" There was only one time I was pushed to use it, and everyone, including 20-year veteran black belts, went silent and stood with attention. There are times when all moms have to flex their voices!

When my daughter left for college, I found myself converting my empty nest energy into nurturing my students. I care for my students, and I am proud to 'mother' them along their journey. I started hosting women's self-defense seminars and diving deeper into my training. I saw the importance of gaining higher ranks so I could be there to represent, not only for the other women and girls, but for anyone who felt small and unsure. I am the tiny, 5'3" woman in a sea of polar bear-sized men who can stand bravely and hold her own among them. It took me 15 years, but I became the first woman to reach third-degree black belt and earn the rank of Sensei, and I got here because I am a mom.

The Japanese have a practice called Kintsugi, where they take something broken such as pottery and repair it with a gold lacquer. The end result is not the same as it was, but rather it is something new and beautiful. We all have times when we feel broken, but with the right tools, you can be repaired and become more beautiful than before.

Valerie Carroll

The very fact that you worry about being a good mother means that you already are one.

Jodi Picoult

Not-Quite-Middle-Aged Shorter-Than-Average Ninja Mama

If my martial arts story had a prologue, mine would take place in the fourth grade during show-and-tell. Larry Davis brought in his karate picture. He was in his karate uniform and doing a full center split and it was so cool! I was already aware of and fascinated by martial arts because that was the height of popularity for the Teenage Mutant Ninja Turtles, but Larry Davis made martial arts real, not just something to watch on screen. It became something I could see myself doing.

I went home and asked my parents if I could train. They told me no, because "girls don't do that."

We fade to black on my prologue scene, and as the lights come back up, we see me in my 20s. I'm married with two boys, Cade and Mason, and boy number three, Tannim, is on the way. The older two trained for a little while in taekwondo with Master John Cooper. I have memories of breastfeeding Tannim while the other two were in class. Oh, and I was working the night shift at the time. When Master Cooper's school had to close, the boys took a break from training as their dad and I turned our attention to other concerns, specifically our failing marriage.

It was a long road that finally led to our decision to split, and in Spring of 2010, I had agreed to remain living in my ex's family home to help take care of the boys. The plan was for me to find my own place and make that crazy transition to a two-home family during the summer break. On May 6, 2010, that plan got thrown out the window.

Before you read any further, please know that my ex-husband and I are on great terms now. A LOT of healing has taken place, and we are in a positive place, co-parenting our boys like champions. Be proud of us for this growth, because we are.

*****I want to preface this next part with a trigger warning for domestic violence. You may wish to skip ahead to the next page.*****

My ex had been experiencing what was presumed at the time to be a bipolar episode. He had been under a lot of stress, and because I was working nights, I was only sleeping two hours a day IF Tannim napped after Mason left for afternoon kindergarten. The ex had car trouble and asked me if I could come pick him up quite a distance away. I was exhausted and could not see. I told him I needed to rest, I was in no state to drive, so I couldn't. He was not happy with this.

Sometime later, after he chose to walk home, he came into the house enraged and saw me napping on the couch. He woke me by shaking me violently and screaming at me about how everything was my fault, I did this to him, I knew his car was going to break down, I'm out to get him, etc.

I found myself grabbed by the shoulders and slammed into the nearest wall. Most of what happened next was a blur … except the look of absolute destruction on ex's face, and the sight of his fist flying toward my face. I ducked just enough that his fist hit the wall behind my head.

Something clicked for him, and he realized that he crossed a line. In that split second, he knew enough to let me go. I took that chance to run next door with his relatives, who were watching Tannim, and called the police. The police came, heard both sides and told me that I needed to leave. It was his house, not mine, so they couldn't make him leave. I was given 10 minutes to grab what I could and go.

*****If you chose to skip the domestic violence section, you can start reading here.*****

I grabbed a few important items, scooped up Tannim, who was not wearing socks, shoes, or pants and may or may not have had a clean diaper at the time, and put him in the car. I drove to the school to pick up my other two boys, and we went to my dad's house.

The shattered pieces of our lives were slowly put back together as we all figured out what the next steps should be. Ultimately, we spent a few months living with my dad until I had the funds to find my own apartment. After my ex spent some time addressing his mental health, he and I agreed on a custody arrangement that would allow us to both be involved in the boys' lives while ensuring the boys stayed in their school with their friends. Life needed to stay as normal as possible during this time. We had enough to worry about.

In January of 2011, my ex and I agreed that it was time to get the boys back into martial arts. We signed them up and agreed on which classes they would attend and who would drive them there. I made sure to be there for every class, even if I had to sit uncomfortably alone in the opposite corner from my ex while things were still strange.

Sometime later, I decided to sign up our youngest son (now four years old) for Little Dragons. The instructor said that I should start training as well. I answered yes with so much enthusiasm that I think I might have scared the instructor a bit. This was the moment I had been waiting for since fourth grade. I was making my own choices, starting a new life for myself, and taking classes would allow me to have a shared activity with my sons. On November 3, 2012, I took my first class. This was the first thing I had done for myself in YEARS.

My boys and I grew a very strong bond. It was great to have something in common that we could talk about and share. Even better, my two oldest sons were senior to me in rank, so I was learning from them. It was like our roles were reversed for the duration of our classes. That taught them a great deal about being respectful and responsible as well as instilling in them that a person's age is not a sign of their competence or leadership abilities. Anyone can do anything, and we shouldn't judge someone by what we see on the outside.

I, too, learned something from this unique experience. I was more willing to take a step back and see the world from my sons' eyes. I didn't run my household like a dictatorship. My kids had a say in the rules, and we were very comfortable discussing issues where we might disagree. We were all on the same level. I was able to share with them my views based on experiences they didn't have, but I also realized that they could do the same. If something would put my kids' health or safety at risk, I might have to put my foot down as their mom, but we always got through our disagreements. Thanks at least in part to this, my kids are comfortable coming to me and talking about difficult topics.

In 2015, my family would be tested again (not in the martial arts sense). My ex was under a lot of stress again, and he was having a hard time functioning. He couldn't take care of himself let alone the boys, and he asked if I could take care of them while he worked on himself. During that time, he and I

agreed that I would keep the boys at my place and get them
to and from school and such so he could heal.

A couple of weeks into the situation, he was still not great,
and he started to fear that he was losing his kids. I offered to
help make arrangements for him to have dinner with the boys
so they could talk, hang out, and ask questions to better
understand what was happening. They needed to know he
was still their dad and that they didn't do anything wrong.
Their dad wanted to think about it.

A few weeks later, the ex started to exhibit the same anger
issues from 2010. I was terrified that we were heading for a
relapse. He would call me and text me to fight with me,
saying I was keeping his kids from him, and I would let him
know that the dinner offer was still on the table, he just
needed to tell me when and where. I informed him that
because of his anger, I was going to attend the dinner to
make sure everyone stayed calm. He did not like that, and he
began making threats against my life. He also threatened me
with legal action, and then he threatened to kidnap the boys
and hide from me so that I would never see them again.

After that last threat, I consulted with a lawyer and began the
custody fight that would encompass the remainder of the
year, and eventually trigger my own mental health crisis that I
still suffer from today. I will not bore you with details of the
court proceedings. No custody battle is a teddy bear picnic,
so you can imagine that there were painful choices and hurt
feelings all around during the next few months.

I struggled. I was encouraged to allow their dad to have
visitation during the custody battle. Every moment the boys
were in his care, I suffered. I was so afraid of what could
happen if he lost control. My boys all trained in martial arts,

but they were still my kids. I hated that I felt like I was not protecting them, and instead putting them in danger every time I dropped them off.

While all of this was happening, we continued to train on our regular schedule. I felt safe in our school, on those mats. It was the only public place I felt comfortable. Everywhere else, I was worried that someone would sneak up behind me and ... bad things. But the dojang was safe. The people there would help us if anyone tried to hurt us. And while we were there, we were learning to be strong and protect ourselves.

I had been training for about 2 1/2 years when this situation began. Suddenly, I was training to save my life and my kids' lives. Every technique took on a new meaning. The way I performed my forms changed. Having all of this going on with my ex gave me something to visualize and FEEL while I trained. That made the difference. For those of you who know me today, you know that I am a big fan of self-defense. This is why.

Early in 2016, the boys' dad and I finally sat down and finalized a custody agreement, with the understanding that if at any time he seemed like he was having another relapse, I would talk to him first before doing anything else … and if he threatened me again, I would do what I needed to do to protect our kids.

The next story centers around boy #2, Mason. He was smart, and he always did a great job when we forced him to sit and do his work, but he didn't do homework without someone nagging him. One assignment in particular that he did not do without pressure was a science fair project. He had a great idea, and he even had the experiment done. He just needed to do the poster explaining his process and results. (Parents, you know the one.) He missed the deadline for turning in the poster, and then he missed the extension deadline. I sat him down, gave him my own deadline, and told him that he would not be allowed to participate in his upcoming belt test if he didn't meet this deadline. Martial artists can't ignore their obligations, and school was (is) important. I needed him to understand that.

In true stubborn Mason fashion, he refused to do the work and the deadline passed. I had a lump in my throat as I told him he couldn't test that month. Because of his advanced rank at the time (2nd gup, testing for 1st gup), not testing meant he was going to need to wait three more months to be eligible to test again. But that's not the worst part. This particular test was pivotal to his progress on the road to black belt. Because of the timing, he was also going to be held back from eligibility for black belt testing for one whole cycle period ... causing him to take a junior position to his older brother for the first time since he began training. Mason lost interest in training from that moment on.

I have regretted that choice for years. I hated watching his heart shatter, and I hated even more that he wanted to quit. I didn't let him quit. I encouraged him to continue training until he reached black belt to see if he still felt the same way. Mason pushed through long enough to earn 2nd Dan before the pandemic hit. When everything shut down, Mason stopped training. I haven't been able to get him to train since. He says it just wasn't his thing, it was more Cade's thing (Cade is my oldest child), and he wanted Cade to have a chance to shine.

Mason was so gifted, though, and he had a certain look in his eye when he was working with other students. I can think of one student in particular that Mason worked with, a student who struggled and with whom many adults had trouble connecting. Mason and this student connected right away. Mason was the only one he could work with, and when Mason explained things to him, he got it right away. Mason was instrumental in this student continuing to train, and that student has achieved a lot in the martial arts, including earning his 1st Dan recently. But Mason wanted to walk away from it all. I can't force him. But, oh, how I miss seeing that look in his eyes.

Tannim later decided to stop training, too. I'm not going to lie. Having two of my boys stop training after we had found martial arts as a way to stay together shattered my world. I am still in denial, telling myself regularly that they will both be back, it's just a break. I know, though, that it is their choice. They will find martial arts again if and when they decide.

I had my daughter in 2020, when I was 40 years old. I didn't know it at the time, but I was pregnant by my final test for second dan in December 2019, and I still passed, "morning" sickness and all. I trained while pregnant with her, and learned just how amazing my body can be. Since the boys had been older when I started training, this was the first time I was faced with the decision of whether or not pregnancy would affect my training. I say "decision," but there was no question for me. Of course, I was going to keep training.

Pregnancy did bring about its own set of challenges for me. I was experiencing "morning" sickness for several months, so bad that I couldn't even drink water. I consulted with my doctor throughout my pregnancy, kept my instructor informed, and stayed safe the whole time. Until the final months, I didn't have to modify much. I reached a point where my body told me to stop doing rolls, then stop doing jumping techniques, and finally, I had so much weight hanging on the front of my body that I needed to do class while seated in a chair and using yoga blocks as supports. (I guess that's funny to me and anyone who knows that I am five feet tall, and when I was pregnant, my belly extended so far forward from my torso that I was wider than I am tall.) I trained until two weeks before Lilith graced us with her presence.

After Lilith was born, I worked on healing so I could return to class as soon as possible. I was finding ways to slow-walk through forms and drills until the doctor cleared me for strenuous activities, and then I was right back in classes. My body recovered quicker from this pregnancy than any of the previous three, and I believe that is because of the martial arts.

By the time I was a third dan, my body was louder when it wanted attention than it was in my 20s. I dealt with burnout constantly, and mood swings, and stress, and anxiety, and I could no longer ignore these messages from my body and mind. I knew I had to take care of myself. I cultivated a daily yoga practice, daily meditation, and found activities that made me happy. I love to cook and bake, read, cross stitch, and solve puzzles. I now have a "rescue tote bag" that goes with me just about everywhere. I keep a book or two, my cross-stitch project, and some puzzle books inside. When I need a break, I reach for my rescue bag and turn my attention inward.

This has been especially helpful with raising my daughter. I have had many a day when I was so stressed out by needing to take care of her needs constantly - she's young, but dang, the toilet training, the feeding, the cleaning, the *Bluey*, all of it is very exhausting for me - that I have forgotten the simple act of drinking water. I would find myself EXTREMELY

thirsty by lunchtime and a headache would start. That's when
I realized that I hadn't done anything for myself all morning.
Time to reach for the rescue tote bag … and a glass of water.

What's the worst that could happen if we don't take care of
ourselves? We could start to fall apart – physically, mentally,
emotionally, spiritually, and any other way you can imagine.
Here's a piece of what happened to me as an example.

Even with my daily yoga practice, etc, I developed anger
issues. There were days when I would snap and yell at the
dumbest stuff. Who put the spoons in the wrong spot in the
dishwasher!? Why is the shower curtain squished aside instead
of open to dry!? Ugh! I forgot to write down that we were out
of chicken nuggets!!

This is where it gets real. I have been a stay-at-home mom
since August of 2021. I thought it would be so much easier to
handle life, the housework, the adult responsibilities, and to
be able to spend quality time with my daughter. I was wrong.

The anger I felt started affecting my relationships, especially
with my daughter. If my kid was excited about something,
and all she wanted to do was get my attention and share it
with me, and I was busy trying to make dinner, I would turn
my attention to her briefly and ask her to leave me alone to
make dinner. I didn't have the mental capacity to handle
playing with her and remember what I was doing in the
kitchen. If she asked me a second or - goodness forbid - a
third time, I would scream at her. She would cry. And not just
any old cry. The cry of "Mommy, you just ripped out my tiny
heart and smashed it into a million pieces. I just want love." It
was NEVER her fault. She is a wonderful, creative,
imaginative, beautiful child. I knew that something was wrong
with me.

I took that cue to find a great therapist. I have been seeing her for two years now, and I have made wonderful progress. Anger management hasn't been my only mental health battle. I also have extreme anxiety and depression. There are times when my anxiety is so crippling that I freeze, forget to breathe, and begin to cry. (Those are stories for another time, though.) I am learning to break that cycle as well, and I have also learned how to accept help from friends as I become a better version of myself. Sidenote: most (not all) of my close friends are amazing people that I have met thanks to the martial arts.

I advocate strongly that mental health IS health, and everyone needs to take a moment and check in with their mental health state from time to time. We deserve to find support in whatever form we need. There should be no stigma around mental health care. It is a necessity. Let's remove the stigma. It's not about being weak. It's about wanting to be stronger.

Today, I am helping my husband accomplish his dream of owning a school. The challenges of being school owners as well as parents have changed how often I can attend classes, but it doesn't affect my ability to train. I make time to train during the day, even if it is just for a few minutes. I'm also grateful that I have help from Mason and Tannim. They watch Lilith while I train on Saturday mornings. My husband teaches, and Cade is in class with me. Cade has also become an extraordinary instructor and has a bright future ahead.

Even after everything I have been through, I feel so strongly that martial arts is the right path for me that no one and nothing can stop me. It's a part of who I am. I feel like the luckiest mom on the planet to have a family who understands this.

It has often been the case that I did not take time to care for myself. There have been days when I have had difficulty in class because my thoughts betrayed me. This has made it difficult to learn new forms or techniques. My body and mind could not get themselves in sync with each other. If I don't take care of myself, I fill my proverbial cup with stress and anxiety and can't hold anything else.

When I was a younger mom with my boys, I was quick to ignore those inner voices who wanted me to take a break. I pushed through and took on too much, and I found myself falling asleep on the couch after dinner quite often because I wasn't nourishing my heart and soul well. I ignored these signals from my body to slow down, and I instead pushed on. Eventually, I would have a mental breakdown or get sick and be forced to stop for a while. I don't ignore these warning signs anymore.

Now, I face daily challenges as the mother of a three-year-old girl. If I feel like I'm having trouble remembering or focusing, I listen to myself. I stop worrying about what needs to be done around the house or next week or whatever, and I do something for myself. Yoga, cross stitching, reading, even something as simple as having a cup of tea and watching a favorite TV show or movie, just enough to take a break and empty that stress-filled cup so I can be ready to take on and share more joy. The best part is that I often find ways to enjoy these self-care activities with my daughter. I'm teaching her to take care of herself now, so hopefully she doesn't forget to take care of herself as she grows up.

I find that training is self-care for me. I may not always feel my best or have lots of energy, but if I take class, I am refreshed, empowered, and ready to get through my day. Plus, if the physical challenges of class are the hardest thing I face all day, and I can push through class, then the day is a win. And if I can face the challenge of class and survive, even with lowered resources, then I can teach myself to face ALL challenges this way.

Even though I push myself to train when I feel less than great, I am not ignoring the days when my body and/or mind say I need a break. I still take time to recover. I have plenty of hobbies that help refill my proverbial cup with joy, and I take time to enjoy them.

I have often found that physical movement helps me release my stress and anxiety. The exercise helps change my thought process, and it helps produce endorphins that support a more positive mood, leaving me feeling more ready to tackle life's challenges after a great class. There are times when I feel stress or anxiety building throughout my day, and I can help re-center myself by taking a moment to do a form or practice some drills of some type. Movement is medicine.

I am more aware of what really matters. It's not about being perfect - the perfect mom, the perfect wife, the perfect daughter, the perfect sister, the perfect whatever. I do what I can, and I prioritize based on my values. I value playtime with my daughter more than I value folding the laundry. If I have managed to find time to clean the laundry but not fold it, that is good enough. I value family time and sharing home-cooked meals more than I value doing dishes, so the dishes might wait until the next morning so we can play a board game together. Our household can operate and the people in it are happy. That is what matters.

I recommend that we all, as moms especially, remember to keep our priorities in check. For example, I still have days where I wish I could finish the dishes and see the bottom of my sink, but I'm spending time with my daughter instead. I have to remember that I'm building memories that will be cherished for a lifetime. I'm playing on the playground, I'm blowing bubbles, I'm dancing and singing as if I'm some famous pop star, I'm getting my butt kicked at Candy Land, and that's just a sample of the memories I'm making with one kid. No one will remember the dishes in the sink, just the joy in the home.

The martial arts taught me to face fear, adversity, and new challenges. They also taught me that we can never be perfect, even though that is our goal. We try our best, and we don't give up. Every day gives us a chance to become better than we used to be.

Being a mother reminds me that I NEED AND WANT to be a positive role model. My kids are watching me, and learning from me. Both on and off the mats, they have seen me struggle, and that taught my kids that we are not perfect, and that's okay. My kids have seen me stop and take time for self-care, and that has taught my kids that we need to remember to love ourselves. My kids have seen me overcome, and that has taught my kids that even when we hit rock bottom, our story isn't over. We can still achieve our goals and live our dreams. I survive for my kids. Because of my kids, I can do anything.

Jenni Nather

If you or someone you know is or may be the victim of a domestic violence situation, help is available.

In my area, we have an organization called The Laurel House. Even if you are not local, this organization can be a great starting place to connect you with organizations where you live or offer advice and counseling.

From their website https://laurel-house.org/:

Do you need help?

Call our 24-hour Hotline:

1-800-642-3150

Or Text "HOPE" to 85511

Laurel House
PO Box 764
Norristown, PA 19404
Office: 610-277-1860
Fax 610-879-2070
info@laurel-house.org

We Want to Hear from You!

Reviews are an important part of how others find our books, and they help us create content you love. If you enjoyed this book, please visit the associated Amazon product listing and leave us a review. We will use your feedback to help create more content catered towards you, our loyal readers.

Thank you!!

DON'T MISS OUR EVENTS!

ALL-IN WEEKEND

This 2-day martial arts event will be half training experience and half retreat. The cost of the event includes all of your training, your lodging, food, and an event shirt. All you have to do is show up, and we'll take care of the rest.

FREE TRAINING DAY

whistlekick's Free Training Day is exactly what the name says - one day of the year where martial artists come together to share and learn, all for free. There is no admission fee at this event, instructors are not paid, and whistlekick picks up the tab for the venue and any other logistical costs.

MARTIAL SUMMIT

Martial Summit is our vision for the future. A place where martial artists, from all over the world, of all systems and styles, come together to share. This 4-day event includes Free Training Day Northeast as well as the Never Settle Awards Banquet.

Follow the QR codes above or visit whistlekick.com and click on "For Individuals" to find all the latest info on our incredible events!

12 Months to Health

This book is designed to help you establish and reinforce 12 simple, inexpensive habits to achieve a healthier you in 12 months.

Available on Amazon now!

"Mr. Lesniak has laid out a well-researched, simple, and gradual guide to real success in incorporating healthy habits into one's daily life. I look forward to sharing this with my patients as a partner in their journey toward better health."

– Joshua Singer, Licensed Acupuncturist at River Street Wellness, Montpelier, Vermont

"Setting just the right goal is hard to do, and starting with consistent, bite-sized, achievable goals is the way to achieve real change in your health."

– Irvin Eisenberg, Masters in Occupational Therapy, Structural Integrator and Owner of Resilience Occupational Therapy

"Our healthcare system, as it is built, right now, is largely not designed to help you until AFTER chronic disease strikes. Even preventative health endorsed by your doctor is left to the small choices you make daily, by yourself, well outside of the walls of the clinic."

– Joshua T. White, MD, MBA, Chief Medical Officer, Gifford Medical Center

"12 things that ANYONE can do that will make a vast difference to their life."

– Daniel Eagles

"A single focus for a month makes it much more likely that I will be able to make sustainable changes."

– StaciAnne KaeLeigh Grove

FREE whistlekick Flexibility Program!

Yes, I said FREE! This program is designed by and for martial artists with features you won't find in any other program, at any price. The Flexibility Program is rooted in the latest science, immensely effective, and different from what most of us were taught.

The FREE whistlekick 30-Day Challenge

The program is a FREE and COMPLETE standalone training program you can start at any time. It's designed to be done on its own, without other strength or conditioning programs. The daily workouts can be completed in about 10 minutes, require NO EQUIPMENT, and can be done in a small indoor space.

This program combines martial arts and fitness to get you the exact workout you need on that day. It helps you build momentum to gain more out of your time – with your health, fitness, training, and the rest of your life.

These are just a sample of the programs we offer!

Looking to increase your speed? How about your fighting endurance? Visit whistlekick.com to see how we are revolutionizing the way you train to improve not only your martial arts skills, but also your overall health.

Check out the collection of whistlekick Programs in the whistlekick Store today!

Did you know whistlekick has a podcast?

We release two episodes each week featuring interviews and topic discussions for the traditional martial artists of the world. You can find more about our *over 900 episodes* at whistlekickmartialartsradio.com.

Some of our past guests include:

Grandmaster Gerald Okamura - Episode 858
Sensei Benny "The Jet" Urquidez - Episode 816
Senior Master of the Arts Jeff Speakman - Episode 802
Mr. Don Wilson - Episode 766
Master Carlos Machado - Episode 714
Shidoshi Ron Van Clief - Episode 698
Mr. Dan Millman - Episode 672
Grandmaster Cynthia Rothrock - Episode 640
Professor Willie "The Bam" Johnson - Episode 636
Dr. Jena Kanokogi - Episode 594
Hanshi Patrick McCarthy - Episode 586
Miss Shannon Lee - Episode 386
Mr. Adrian Paul - Episode 380
Shihan Bas Rutten - Episode 362
Coach Kathy Long - Episode 274
Shihan Chris Casamassa - Episode 216
Mr. Iain Abernethy - Episode 186
Grandmaster Jhoon Rhee - Episode 180
Sensei Jesse Enkamp - Episode 174
Coach Daniel Wu - Episode 171
Sensei Fumio Demura - Episode 130
Mr. Tony Blauer - Episode 108
Kyoshi Dave Kovar - Episode 29
Bill "Superfoot" Wallace - Episode 14

We Truly Appreciate You!

Thank you for supporting whistlekick Books. We invite you to visit us at whistlekick.com. While there, you will find links to check out our other books, our store, social media, how to leave us reviews, info on our other projects, and much more.

We are always open to your thoughts, questions, and suggestions. You may contact us anytime at books@whistlekick.com.

Thank you!

wK Books